# BIRNBAUM'S GUIDES

## 2010

# Walt Disney World
## POCKET PARKS GUIDE

**Wendy Lefkon** EDITORIAL DIRECTOR

**Jill Safro** EDITOR

**Debbie Lofaso** DESIGNER

**Jessica Ward** ASSISTANT EDITOR

**Alexandra Mayes Birnbaum** CONSULTING EDITOR

THE OFFICIAL GUIDE

---

**Stephen Birnbaum** FOUNDING EDITOR

Expert Advice from the Inside Source

DISNEY EDITIONS

NEW YORK
AN IMPRINT OF DISNEY BOOK GROUP

**For Steve, who merely made all this possible**

## Other 2010 Birnbaum's Official Disney Guides

*Disney Cruise Line*
*Disneyland Resort*
*Walt Disney World*
*Walt Disney World Dining*
*Walt Disney World For Kids*
*Walt Disney World Without Kids*

# Table of Contents

# A Word from the Editor

**H**oney, we shrunk the Birnbaum Guide! Yep, it's true. In response to pleas from readers like you, we proudly present our *Official Pocket Guide to Walt Disney World Parks.* A parks-only guide is a practical companion to the comprehensive WDW–vacation planner known as *Birnbaum's Official Guide to Walt Disney World.* Why? Once you've arrived in Walt's World, arranging that hassle-free vacation is a thing of the past, and the new focus is exclusively on fun. So, consider this

Editor Jill Safro consults with Mickey and Minnie, the ultimate Disney insiders.

the "We've done our homework and now it's time to play!" guide. Drop your bags, pop this book into a pocket, and make a beeline for your favorite Disney park.

Just as with the meticulously detailed "big guide"—which we recommend you stash by your bedside in your resort room—this book has obsessively researched, as-current-as-possible information on all four Walt Disney World theme parks and both water parks. We've included a thorough description of every show and attraction the World has to offer, as well as time-tested sample schedules—conveniently perforated so you can store them in your pocket. Further, we've added our "Birnbaum's Best" seal of approval to attractions we believe stand head, shoulders, and ears above the rest. And, of course, we've included scads of our famous

Hot Tips throughout the book. Used in conjunction with park guidemaps and Times Guides (available for free at all Walt Disney World resorts and parks), this expert information will help you get the most bang for your theme-park-ticket buck. (Note that Times Guides are park-specific, one-sheet bulletins that are chock-full of useful information. Refer to them for attraction schedules, parade and fireworks presentation times, character appearances schedules, and more.) Another valuable reference tool is the soon-to-be personalized Trip Tracker. It is the perfect place to record confirmation numbers, restaurant reservations, park-hopping strategies, and more. (You'll find it on page 117.)

Perhaps the most enjoyable reason to take us along with you? We've stuffed this guide with dozens upon dozens of "Hidden Mickeys" for your sleuthing pleasure. What's a Hidden Mickey? It's an image of the Mouse that has been strategically "hidden" by Disney Imagineers. Some are easy to spot, others not so much. We'll help you discover a whole bunch of them. It's just another layer of fun to add to a walk in the park.

As a final bonus, we have provided a handy pocket in which to store those precious Fastpass slips. Not familiar with Fastpass? It's Disney's almost too-good-to-be-true system that allows guests to bypass long lines *for free*. Read about it

### Disney World Digits

Information and ticket sales: 407-824-4321
Lost and Found: 407-824-4245
Recreation reservations: 407-939-7529
Resort reservations: 407-934-7639
Restaurant reservations: 407-939-3463

on the inside front cover and use Fastpass as often as you can.

Finally, it is important to remember that every worthwhile travel guide is a living enterprise: The book you hold in your hands is our best effort at explaining how to enjoy Walt Disney World theme parks and water parks, but it is in no way etched in stone. As we direct our efforts to updating this "pocket" book for 2011, we will continue to refine our efforts to serve your needs better and demonstrate that good things do, indeed, come in small packages.

Have a great time in the parks!

## Don't Forget to Write

No contribution is of greater value to us in preparing the next edition of this book than your comments on what we have written and on your own experiences at Walt Disney World. Please share your insights with us by writing to:

**Jill Safro, Editor**
***Birnbaum's Walt Disney World***
  ***Pocket Parks Guide 2010***
**Disney Editions**
**114 Fifth Avenue, 14th Floor**
**New York, NY 10011**

# Magic Kingdom

The Magic Kingdom is the most enchanting part of the World. Few who visit it are disappointed, and even the most blasé travelers manage a smile. The sight of the soaring spires of Cinderella Castle, the gleaming woodwork of the Main Street shops, and the crescendo of music that follows the parades never fails to have its effect. Even when the crowds are large and the weather is hot, a visitor who has toured this wonderland dozens of times can still look around and think how satisfying this place is for the spirit.

What makes the Magic Kingdom timeless is its combination of the classic and the futuristic. Both childhood favorites and space-age creatures have a home here. Every "land" has a theme, carried through from the costumes worn by the hosts and hostesses and the food served in the restaurants to the merchandise sold in the shops, and even the design of the trash cans. Thousands of details contribute to the overall effect, and recognizing these touches makes any visit more enjoyable.

But the delight most guests experience upon first glimpse of the Magic Kingdom can disappear when disorientation sets in. There are so many bends to every pathway, so many sights and sounds clamoring for attention, it's too easy to wander aimlessly and miss the best the Magic Kingdom has to offer. So we earnestly suggest that you refer to this chapter during your visit.

# Getting Oriented

When you visit Walt Disney World's original theme park, it's vital to know the lay of the "lands." The Magic Kingdom has seven lands—Main Street, U.S.A.; Adventureland; Frontierland; Liberty Square; Fantasyland; Mickey's Toontown Fair; and Tomorrowland. Main Street begins at Town Square, located just inside the park gates, and runs directly to Cinderella Castle. The area in front of the castle is known as the Central Plaza or the Hub. Bridges over the waterways here serve as passages to each of the lands.

## HOW TO GET THERE

**By car:** Take Exit 64B off I-4. Continue about four miles to the Auto Plaza and park; walk or take a tram to the main entrance complex, known as the Transportation and Ticket Center (TTC). Choose a 7-minute ferry ride or a slightly shorter trip by monorail for the last leg of an anticipation-filled journey.

**By WDW Transportation:** From the Grand Floridian and Polynesian: monorail or boat. From the Contemporary: monorail or walkway. (It is about a 10- to 15-minute stroll.) From Epcot: monorail to the Transportation and Ticket Center (TTC), then transfer to the Magic Kingdom monorail or ferry. From Disney's Hollywood Studios, Animal Kingdom, and the resorts on Hotel Plaza Boulevard: buses to the TTC, then transfer to ferry or monorail. From Fort Wilderness: boat or bus. From Disney's Wilderness Lodge: boat or bus. From Downtown Disney: bus to any Disney resort and transfer to the Magic Kingdom bus (or monorail). From all other Disney resorts: buses.

## PARKING

All-day parking at the Magic Kingdom is $12 for day visitors (free to Disney World resort guests with a valid resort ID or an annual pass).

## GETTING AROUND

Walt Disney World Railroad trains make a loop of the park, with stations on Main Street, Frontierland, and Mickey's Toontown Fair. Classic vehicles offer one-way trips down Main Street.

# Park Primer

## BABY FACILITIES

The best place in the Magic Kingdom to take care of little ones' needs is the Baby Care Center. This cheery site, equipped with changing tables and facilities for nursing mothers, is located next to the Crystal Palace restaurant. Disposable diapers are for sale at many Magic Kingdom shops (they're kept behind the counter, just ask). All park restrooms have changing facilities.

## CAMERA NEEDS

The Camera Center in the Town Square Exposition Hall proffers memory cards and disposable cameras, plus film and batteries. It's also possible to make prints and transfer images from your media card to a CD. This is also where you can view and/or purchase photos shot by Disney's PhotoPass photographers. (If you'd rather wait till you get home to check out your photos, visit *www.disneyphotopass.com*. Don't forget to keep your PhotoPass card handy!)

## DISABILITY INFORMATION

Most Magic Kingdom shops and restaurants, and many attractions, are accessible to guests using wheelchairs. Additional services are available for guests with visual or hearing disabilities. The *Guide for Guests with Disabilities* provides an overview of all services available. For a copy, or to address a specific concern, visit Guest Relations or City Hall.

## FERRY VERSUS MONORAIL

For guests arriving by car or bus, it's necessary to decide whether to travel to the Magic Kingdom by ferry or monorail. The monorail makes the trip from the Transportation and Ticket Center (TTC) in about five minutes while the ferry takes about seven. During busy seasons, the ferry will often get you there faster (long lines can form at the monorail, and most people don't make the short walk to the ferry landing). Vacationers who use wheelchairs should note that while the monorail platforms are accessible, the ramp leading to the boarding area is a bit on the steep side.

## FIRST AID

A registered nurse tends to minor medical problems at the First Aid Center, located near the Crystal Palace restaurant.

## INFORMATION

City Hall, just inside the park entrance, serves as the Magic Kingdom's information headquarters. Guest Relations representatives can answer questions. Guidemaps and Times Guides, updated weekly (including details about entertainment, as well as character greeting times and locations), are available here, and all kinds of arrangements can be made, including reservations for restaurants.

## LOCKERS

Attended lockers are located just inside the park entrance, all the way to the right. Lockers are also available at the Transportation and Ticket Center (TTC). If you "hop" to another park on the same day, you don't have to pay to get another locker. Simply present your receipt to the attendant and you're all set.

## LOST & FOUND

On the day of your visit, report lost articles at City Hall or at the TTC. Recovered items can also be claimed at these locations. After your visit, call 407-824-4245. To make matters easier, we suggest affixing contact info to your camera. (We learned that the hard way!)

## LOST CHILDREN

Report lost children at City Hall or the Baby Care Center, and alert a Disney employee to the problem.

## MONEY MATTERS

The Magic Kingdom has four Automated Teller machines (ATMs). Check a guidemap for locations. Credit cards (American Express, Visa, MasterCard, JCB, Discover Card, Diner's Club, Disney gift cards, and the Disney Visa Card) are accepted as payment for admission, merchandise, and meals at all full-service restaurants and fast-food locations. Traveler's checks and Walt Disney World resort ID cards are also accepted in most places. Some food and souvenir carts accept cash only.

Disney Dollars are available at City Hall (as well as World of Disney at Downtown Disney) in $1, $5, and $10 denominations. They are accepted for dining and merchandise throughout most of WDW and can be exchanged at any time for U.S. currency. Gift cards (from $5 to $1,500) may be purchased at most shops.

## PACKAGE PICKUP

Shops can arrange for purchases of any size to be transported to Package Pickup on Main Street, next to City Hall, for pickup between noon and park closing time (at least three hours after purchase). Packages may be sent to Disney resorts, too. The service is free.

## SAME-DAY RE-ENTRY

Retain your ticket if you plan to return later the same day. A hand stamp is no longer required for re-entry.

## SECURITY CHECK

Guests entering Disney theme parks are subject to a security check. Backpacks, parcels, purses, etc. will be searched by Disney security personnel before guests are permitted to pass through the turnstiles.

## STROLLERS & WHEELCHAIRS

Wheelchair Rental, located just inside the turnstiles, all the way to the right, offers wheelchairs (some over-sized) and Electric Convenience Vehicles (ECVs). Strollers are available under the Main Street Train Station. Quantities are limited. Hold on to your receipt; it can be used on the same day to get a replacement stroller or wheelchair at any of the theme parks. Multi-day rentals, called Length of Stay tickets, save a bit off the daily price. Keep your receipt handy.

**Note:** Given that the strollers here cannot be removed from the park and are made of hard plastic, many guests choose to save a few bucks by bringing a stroller from home.

## TIP BOARD

Located at the end of Main Street, U.S.A., closest to Cinderella Castle, the Tip Board is an excellent source of information on waiting times for attractions, as well as showtimes and other entertainment information. The board is often overseen by a park-savvy employee, ready and willing to answer guest questions.

# Main Street, U.S.A.

Stepping onto Main Street, U.S.A., is like jumping through a time portal. The street represents an ideal American town of yesteryear. Although such a town may never have existed, many claim to have served as the inspiration for it. Chances are Walt Disney got the idea from Marceline, Missouri,

the tiny rural town that was his boyhood home.

Once you start to meander along Main Street, be sure to notice the names on the second-story windows. They all belong to folks connected with The Walt Disney Company. (Look for Walt's name above the ice cream parlor.)

**WALT DISNEY WORLD RAILROAD:** The 1½-mile journey on this rail line is as much a must for the first-time visitor as it is for railroad buffs.

The train circles the park in about 20 minutes, making stops in Frontierland, Mickey's Toontown Fair, and Main Street, U.S.A. Trains usually arrive in each station every 4 to 10 minutes. The line is generally the shortest in Toontown, but there's rarely a long wait at any of the stations. The train is the best way to reach the exit when parades take over the park.

**Note:** The Walt Disney World Railroad does not run during fireworks presentations.

**MAIN STREET VEHICLES:** A number of these can be seen traveling up and down Main Street—horseless carriages and jitneys patterned after turn-of-the-century vehicles; a spiffy scarlet fire engine; and a troop of trolleys drawn by Belgians and Percherons, two strong breeds of horse that once pulled plows in Europe. They relax in the Car Barn in between shifts. Stop by and say hello!

**TOWN SQUARE EXPOSITION HALL:** A veritable shrine to photography, Town Square Exposition Hall does double duty as a museum and camera-supply shop. Be sure to take your own camera, as photo ops abound.

# Adventureland

Surrounded by tropical splendor, this area has the look and feel of a bustling marketplace—the likes of which one might stumble upon in Agrabah. The shops  here offer imports from around the globe.

**SWISS FAMILY TREEHOUSE:** This is everybody's idea of the perfect treehouse, with its many levels and comforts—patchwork quilts, mahogany furniture, candles stuck in abalone shells, even running water in every room. Based on the wondrous banyan-tree home in Disney's 1960 rendition of the classic story *Swiss Family Robinson*, it rarely fails to intrigue. The only modern convenience the Robinsons could use? An elevator! Expect to burn off a few calories climbing up and down the stairs.

The Spanish moss draping the branches is real; the tree itself—unofficially christened *Disneyodendron eximus*, a genus that is translated roughly as "out-of-the-ordinary Disney tree"—was constructed by the props department.

**JUNGLE CRUISE:** **FP** Inspired in part by the 1955 documentary film *The African Lion*, this 9-minute adventure is one of the crowning achievements of Magic Kingdom landscape artists for the way it takes guests through surroundings as diverse as a Southeast Asian jungle, the Nile Valley, and an Amazon rainforest. Along the way, passengers encounter zebras, giraffes, lions, headhunters, and more (all of the Audio-Animatronics variety); they also see elephants bathing and tour a temple—while listening to an amusing, if corny, spiel delivered by the skipper.

This adventure, which is best enjoyed by daylight, is one of the park's slower-moving attractions, and tends to be quite crowded from late morning until late afternoon.

**THE ENCHANTED TIKI ROOM—UNDER NEW MANAGEMENT:** The Tiki Birds are legends in their own time. Yet, the cherished stars of the world's first Audio-Animatronics attraction fell into a bit of a rut a few years back. Now, thanks to clever new costars and zippy new tunes, the Tiki Room is rockin' once again. The 20-minute show, which features some 200 birds, flowers, and tikis, does have its dark moments (courtesy of an angry tiki god), which may frighten small children.

**THE MAGIC CARPETS OF ALADDIN:** Welcome to Agrabah! This 2-minute ride features not one, but 16 carpets that fly through the air in a fashion similar to those airborne elephants over in Fantasyland. Each flying carpet accommodates four guests at a time. Depending on where you sit, you'll have control of the carpet's vertical movement (the controls are in the front). Be prepared to dodge the occasional stream of liquid, courtesy of an expectorating camel.

**BIRNBAUM'S ★BEST★** **PIRATES OF THE CARIBBEAN:** Quite simply, this is one of the very best of the Magic Kingdom's classic adventures. The beloved 9-minute cruise is a Disneyland original, added to Walt Disney World's Magic Kingdom (in slightly revised form) due to popular demand. Here, guests board a small boat and set sail for a series of scenes showing a pirate raid on a Caribbean island town, dodging cannon fire and weathering one small, though legitimate, watery dip along the way.

While it's by no means politically correct (far from it, actually), the rendition of "Yo Ho, Yo Ho, a Pirate's Life for Me"—the catchy theme song—makes what is actually a rather brutal scenario into something that comes across as good fun.

There are singing marauders, plastered pigs, and wily wenches; the observant may note a couple of familiar rapscallion residents. Yep, that beloved scallywag Captain Jack Sparrow has dropped anchor here, as has his nefarious nemesis, Captain Barbossa.

# Frontierland

With the Rivers of America lapping at its borders and Big Thunder Mountain rising up in the rear, this re-creation of the American frontier encompasses the area from New England to the Southwest, from the  1770s to the 1880s. The Walt Disney World Railroad makes a stop here.

**FRONTIERLAND SHOOTIN' ARCADE:** This modest arcade is set in an 1850s town in the Southwest Territory. Positions overlook Boothill, a town complete with bank, jail, hotel, and cemetery.

It is possible to have fun here, but this arcade is in dire need of an upgrade. There is an additional charge to play here (about 50 cents).

**COUNTRY BEAR JAMBOREE:** The Country Bears may never make it to the Grand Ole Opry, but they don't seem to mind. Disney's brood of banjo-strummin' bruins has been playing to packed houses in Grizzly Hall for more than a quarter century. Judging by all the toe tappin' and hand clappin' that accompany each performance, the show remains a countrified crowd-pleaser. As for the few folks who aren't charmed by the backwoods ballads and down-home humor, well, they just have to grin and *bear* it.

**Timing Tip:** This 16-minute attraction opens at 10 A.M. each day, even when the rest of the park opens earlier.

**TOM SAWYER ISLAND:** This patch of land in the middle of the Rivers of America has hills to scramble up; a working windmill, Harper's Mill, with an owl in the rafters and a perpetually creaky waterwheel; and a few pitch-black caves. To reach the island, guests take a raft across the river. (It's the only way to get there and back.)

Paths wind this way and that, and it's easy to get disoriented. Keep an eye out for mounted maps scattered about the island.

There are two bridges here—a suspension bridge and a barrel bridge that floats atop some lashed-together wooden barrels. Across the suspension bridge is Fort Langhorn. Poke around and you'll discover a twisting, dark, and occasionally scary escape tunnel.

The whole island seems as rugged as backwoods Missouri, and probably as a result, it actually feels a lot more remote than it is—enough to be able to provide some welcome respite from the bustle. (Restrooms are beside the main raft landing and inside Fort Langhorn.)

**Timing Tip:** This attraction closes at dusk.

**BIRNBAUM'S ★BEST★ SPLASH MOUNTAIN: FP** In this guaranteed smile-inducer, guests enjoy an 11-minute waterborne (potentially drenching) journey through swamps and bayous and down waterfalls, and are finally hurtled from the peak of the mountain to a briar-laced pond five stories below.

Splash Mountain is based on the animated sequences in Walt Disney's 1946 film *Song of the South*. The scenery entertains as the story line follows Br'er Rabbit as he tries to reach his "laughin' place." It's tough for a first-time rider to take in all the details, since the tension of waiting for the big drop is all-consuming.

It is a bit terrifying at the top, but once back on the ground, it seems most riders can't wait for another trip—even though they may get drenched. (Water-wary guests are often seen wearing rain ponchos on this attraction. On the other hand, if you *want* to get wet, try to sit up front or on the right; seats in the back receive a slightly smaller splash.)

**Note:** The minimum height requirement is 40 inches. (There is a small play area nearby to keep little ones occupied while older kids ride.) If you'd like to absorb as little precipitation as possible, sit on the left side of the log.

**BIRNBAUM'S** **BIG THUNDER MOUNTAIN RAILROAD:**
**★BEST★** FP According to Disney legend, the
2½-acre mountain is chock-full of gold.
Unfortunately for the residents of Tumbleweed, the local
mining town, a flood has ruined any chance of uncovering the remaining gold. Before these prospectors find
drier land, they are having one last party at the saloon to
celebrate their riches. Even though in danger of washing
away, they don't seem too worried, and guests who
decide to take a trip on the Big Thunder Mountain
Railroad have nothing to worry about either.

As passengers board the 15-row train, they are advised
to "hang on to your hats and glasses 'cause this here's
the wildest ride in the wilderness." Do heed the warning,
but don't despair. The 3½-minute ride, though thrilling,
is relatively tame, so relax and enjoy the sights. Note
that passengers seated nearest the caboose experience
more turbulence than those
up front.

A continuous string of
curves and dips around Big
Thunder's pinnacles and
caverns is sure to please
thrill seekers of all ages,
but the adrenaline surge is
caused by more than just
the speed of the trip. The
added sound of a rickety
track, a steam whistle that
blows right before the train
accelerates into a curve,
and a minor earthquake all
compound the passengers'
anticipation, making this
attraction one of the Magic
Kingdom's most popular.

**Note:** You must be immune to motion sickness to
experience the Big Thunder Mountain Railroad attraction. Minimum height requirement: 40 inches.

**Timing Tip:** Plan to visit early in the morning, during a
parade, or just before closing time. Of course, you can
always plan ahead and get a Fastpass. If you will be visiting during a parade, consider taking the Walt Disney
World Railroad to the Frontierland station. The train
circumvents much of the parade congestion.

# Liberty Square

The transition between Frontierland on one side and Fantasyland on the other is so smooth that it's hard to say just when you arrive at Liberty Square, yet ultimately there's no mistaking the location. It truly is Americana central. There's even a replica of the Liberty Bell!

**THE HALL OF PRESIDENTS:** This spruced up, 23-minute classic is long on patriotism and short on silliness. After a film (which is presented on a sweeping 70mm screen) discusses the importance of the relationship between the role of the presidency and the American people, the curtain goes up, revealing a cast of American leaders. All 44 chief executives are represented by Audio-Animatronics likenesses.

   **Timing Tip:** Planning to visit the Presidents? This attraction opens at 10 A.M., even when the rest of the park opens earlier. It often closes before the park does. The show usually starts on the hour and half hour.

**LIBERTY BELLE RIVERBOAT:** Based in Liberty Square and built in dry dock at Walt Disney World, this is a real steamboat. Its boiler turns water into steam, which is then piped to the engine, which drives the paddle wheel that propels the boat. It is not the real article in one respect, however:

It moves through the nine-foot-deep Rivers of America on an underwater rail.

The pleasant ride, with narration by an actor playing Mark Twain, is a good way to escape the masses for a bit. En route, a variety of props create a sort of Wild West effect: moose, deer, a burning cabin, and the like. The tour is completed within 17 minutes.

**BIRNBAUM'S ★BEST★ THE HAUNTED MANSION:** This 7½-minute experience is among the Magic Kingdom's most enjoyable. However, guests who expect to be scared silly when they enter the big old house, modeled after those built in New York's Hudson River Valley in the 18th century, will be just a tad unfulfilled. This haunted house steers clear of anything too terrifying. WDW vets might notice a few enhancements to the manse—including a new room filled with "stairs to nowhere."

Once you're inside the portrait hall, it's amusing to speculate: Is the ceiling moving up, or is the floor dropping? It's also where you meet your "Ghost Host" and learn how he met his untimely demise. The inky darkness may startle tots.

The spooky journey through the mansion takes place in a "Doom Buggy." The attraction is full of tricks and treats for the eyes; just when you think you've seen it all, there's something new: bats' eyes on the wallpaper, a terrified cemetery watchman and his mangy mutt, and the image of a creepy lady in a floating crystal ball.

One of the biggest jobs of the maintenance crews here is not cleaning up, but keeping things dirty. The mansion is littered with some 200 trunks, chairs, dress forms, harps, rugs, and assorted knick-knacks, and requires a lot of dust. Cobwebs are bought in liquid

form and strung up by a secret process.

On the way out, take a moment to pay your respects at the pet cemetery. We miss you, Mr. Toad! Sniff, sniff.

# Fantasyland

Walt Disney called this a "timeless land of enchantment," and his successors termed it "the happiest land of all"—and it is, for some. Kids love it here.

**CINDERELLA CASTLE:**
Just as Mickey stands for all
the merriment in Walt Disney World, this storybook castle represents the hopes and dreams of childhood—a time when anything is possible.

Unlike real European castles, this 190-foot replica is made of steel and fiberglass; in lieu of dungeons, it has service tunnels. Its upper reaches contain security rooms; there's even a special Cinderella Castle Suite. It was created to fulfill guests' dreams during the "Year of a Million Dreams" Celebration. (Future plans for this spectacular space were undetermined at press time. Though we will happily volunteer to move in.) From any vantage point, Cinderella Castle looks as if it came straight from the land of make-believe.

**Bibbidi Bobbidi Boutique:** Tucked inside Cinderella Castle, this shop offers young guests the opportunity to be transformed into "little princesses" and princely "cool dudes." Magical makeovers are available from 8 A.M. to 7 P.M. Prices vary. Magic Kingdom admission is required to enter this location.

**Mosaic Murals:** The elaborate murals beneath the castle's archway rank among the true wonders of the World. They tell the story of the little cinder girl and one of childhood's happiest happily-ever-afters using a million bits of glass in some 500 different colors, plus real silver and gold.

**Cinderella Wishing Well:** This pleasant alcove, nestled along a path to Tomorrowland, is a nice spot from which to gaze at the castle. Any coins tossed into the water are donated to children's charities. Don't forget to make a wish as you part with your penny.

**CINDERELLA'S GOLDEN CARROUSEL:** Discovered at the now-defunct Olympic Park in Maplewood, New Jersey, this carrousel was built in 1917. That was the end of the golden century of carrousel building. The 2-minute ride is favored by guests of all ages.

**FAIRYTALE GARDEN:** This special corner of the Kingdom is tucked beside Cinderella Castle. Several times a day, Belle stops by to read a story and, afterward, mingle with guests. There are about 20 seats — to snag one, arrive early.

**MICKEY'S PHILHARMAGIC:** **FP** Mickey Mouse and pals (including Donald, Simba, and Ariel) strut their musical stuff in this ear- and eye-popping production.

The 12-minute show is an ambitious amalgam of music, special effects, and animated film. Of course, this being Fantasyland, the film is by no means ordinary. It's crisp, colorful, and, to the delight of many a goggle-wearing guest, three-dimensional. The 3-D experience unfolds on a 150-foot-wide canvas, which is one of the largest screens ever created for a film of this kind.

As with many attractions, there may be occasional moments of darkness. If you're unsure as to whether your child might find this (or any attraction) unsettling, express your concern to an attendant. They'll help you make the right decision.

**BIRNBAUM'S** **★BEST★** **PETER PAN'S FLIGHT:** **FP** The 3-minute adventure, which takes you soaring in a pirate ship, fancifully retells the story of Peter Pan — a boy with a knack for flying and an immunity to maturity. The effects in this Fantasyland classic are simple, but enchanting. Hence, it is one of the most popular attractions in the park. Get a Fastpass if you can.

**IT'S A SMALL WORLD:** Originally created for New York's 1964–65 World's Fair, the 10-minute attraction is an oldie-but-goodie (and is quite popular with young children). The ride moves at slightly swifter than snail's pace, drifting past hundreds of colorfully costumed dolls from around the world — all of whom know all the words to the ride's infectious theme song (a singsong melody which reminds us that it's a small world after all). The attraction is a simple celebration of human similarities. It's also a relaxing alternative to many of the park's higher-tech, longer-line attractions.

**DUMBO THE FLYING ELEPHANT:** This is purely and simply a kiddie ride, though children of all ages have admitted to loving it. A beloved symbol of Fantasyland, it's most popular with the 2-to-8-year-old set. Inspired by the 1941 film classic *Dumbo*, the ride lasts two minutes.

**MAD TEA PARTY:** The theme of this 2-minute ride — in a group of oversize pastel-colored teacups that whirl and spin wildly—was inspired by a scene in the Disney Studios' 1951 production of *Alice in Wonderland*. Unlike many rides in Fantasyland, this is not just for younger kids; the 9-to-20-something crowd seems to like it best. Skip this ride if you suffer from motion sickness or if you've recently enjoyed a snack.

**BIRNBAUM'S** **★BEST★** **THE MANY ADVENTURES OF WINNIE THE POOH:** FP The 3½-minute experience features a most unlikely form of transportation: honey pots! They whisk (and bounce) guests through the pages of a storybook and into the Hundred Acre Wood, where the weather's most blustery. Sight gags abound, from a bubble-blowing Heffalump (hey, this is Fantasyland) to a treacherous flood that threatens to sweep Tigger, Piglet, and the rest of the gang away. When Pooh saves the day, it's time to celebrate—and everyone is invited to the party.

Note that some parts of The Many Adventures of Winnie the Pooh take place in the dark. Timid youngsters may find it a bit unsettling.

**POOH'S PLAYFUL SPOT:** A patch of the Hundred Acre Wood has sprung up in Fantasyland, just across the way from The Many Adventures of Winnie the Pooh. Geared toward very young guests, this simple, soft-surface play zone has logs to climb on, a treehouse to explore, plus honey pots, a slide, and more.

**SNOW WHITE'S SCARY ADVENTURES:** This 3-minute attraction takes guests on a twisting, turning journey through a few happy moments and several scary scenes from the famous fairy tale (and the world's first full-length animated feature). Snow White makes several appearances, as do the Seven Dwarfs. But the wicked witch pops up with a suddenness that freaks out some kids (mostly those under the age of 5).

# Mickey's Toontown Fair

This colorful neighbor-
hood was built with
little visitors in mind.
Not only do Mickey,
Minnie, and their pals
keep homes here, but
the county fair is
always in town. Tucked
away behind Fantasy-

land, the area can be reached by a path from the Mad
Tea Party or Space Mountain and via the Walt Disney
World Railroad. Guests who arrive by stroller are
advised to park their vehicles in the lot across from
Pete's Garage. Traffic here is heaviest early in the day.

**THE BARNSTORMER AT GOOFY'S WISEACRE
FARM:** At this mini roller coaster attraction, guests of
most sizes climb into crop dusters and follow the same
fluky flight path taken by the Goof himself. The planes
zip through the farm and crash through a barn, causing
quite a ruckus among the chickens. Don't let the size
fool you: This 1-minute ride proves that big thrills
come in small packages. Although guests as young as 3
are allowed to ride, they must be at least 35 inches tall.
It may be too turbulent for some.

**DONALD'S BOAT:** If you want to cool off a bit, stop
at Donald Duck's boat, the *Miss Daisy*. The vessel has
sprung so many leaks, it looks like a fountain. The
ship's sparse interior includes a captain's wheel and a
whistle—pull it and water shoots out the top. Tykes
love it. Waterproof diapers are a must.

**MICKEY'S COUNTRY HOUSE:** Don't bother knock-
ing—the door is always open. Guests are welcome to
peer inside each of the cottage's rooms: bedroom, living room, kitchen, and game room. The screen porch is
full of some very special plants. Don't miss the palm
tree (it's made of hands), the Tiger Lilies (feline faces),
and the Twolips (no explanation necessary).

**JUDGE'S TENT:** A must for fans of the Mouse, this
place is all Mickey all the time. (To get there, slip out

the back door of Mickey's house and follow the path toward the tent.) The waiting area—and there is almost always a significant wait—features a pre-show video that highlights all of his county fair successes. All guests are treated to a private meeting with the star, so have those cameras ready! (The only way to get to the Judge's Tent is by taking a trip through Mickey's House.) The line is usually shortest late in the day or during a parade.

**TOONTOWN HALL OF FAME:** Just beyond Cornelius Coot Commons and across from Goofy's Wiseacre Farm is the Toontown Hall of Fame. Beyond the retail area, three different rooms offer guests the opportunity to meet Disney characters.

There is a separate line for each room, and characters vary throughout the day. One of the rooms is dedicated to Disney princesses. Another room, called Pixie Hollow, lets guests mingle with Tinker Bell and her fairy friends. Expect characters in the third room to vary. Have those cameras (and autograph books) ready!

**MINNIE'S COUNTRY HOUSE:** Minnie's house is merely a hop, skip, and a jump from Mickey's. Young kids love it here because the special toon furniture is meant for climbing. As they explore, guests may push a button to listen to her answering-machine messages, open the refrigerator, and try in vain to snatch some chocolate chip cookies. (It's a mirror trick, courtesy of Minnie herself. She's one clever mouse.)

**PETE'S PAINT SHOP:** Feeling frisky? For about $15, you can have your face painted like a tiger. Other choices include chipmunk, pirate, superhero, and evil queen.

**TOON PARK:** Centrally located, this covered green provides a nice respite from the sun (or the rain).

# Tomorrowland

This is the future that never was, the fantasy world imagined by the science-fiction writers and moviemakers of the 1920s and '30s. It's a land of sky-piercing beacons and glistening metal, where shiny robots do the work, whisper-quiet cars glide along an elevated highway, and even time travel is possible.

**STITCH'S GREAT ESCAPE!:** FP This attraction features the adventures of a renegade alien. Fortunately, said extraterrestrial is more of a menace than a threat—not so much scary as ill-mannered and mischievous. The 18-minute show is a prequel to *Lilo & Stitch*, but one need not be familiar with the drooling, intergalactic imp to follow the attraction's story line.

The action begins with a short pre-show, followed by the crowd spilling into a circular theater-type room. All chairs face center, where there's a mysterious tube. (Sit up straight when the shoulder harness is lowered—this will enhance the effects.) The attraction tends to be best appreciated by Stitch groupies.

**Note:** Some youngsters may be frightened by dark moments and loud noises. Also, shoulder restraints may spook claustrophobes. You must be at least 40 inches tall to enter.

**BIRNBAUM'S ★BEST★ BUZZ LIGHTYEAR'S SPACE RANGER SPIN:** FP The evil Emperor Zurg is up to no good. As soon as he swipes enough batteries to power his ultimate weapon of destruction—KERPLOOEY!—it's curtains for the toy universe as we know it. It's up to that Space Ranger extraordinaire Buzz Lightyear and his Junior Space Rangers (that means you) to save the day.

FP = FASTPASS ATTRACTION

Will good prevail over evil? Or has time run out for the toy universe? And will you score enough points to be a Galactic Hero? (Most people improve their scores with a little practice.)

**MONSTERS, INC. LAUGH FLOOR:** That Mike Wazowski is one enterprising eyeball. It seems the fuzzy fellow from *Monsters, Inc.* has opened something of a comedy club. Why? Well, it seems his hometown is experiencing an energy crisis. Mike's plan is to tap into an alternative (not to mention free) fuel source to provide power for Monstropolis . . . laughter. To accomplish his goal, Monster of Ceremonies Mike has recruited a couple of cornball comedians. Their job is to make you chuckle for 11 minutes. Expect to grin, grimace, and hopefully, guffaw. At press time, it was possible to send Mike your favorite joke via text message. Who knows? Maybe yours will make it into the show!

**TOMORROWLAND TRANSIT AUTHORITY:** Boarded near Astro Orbiter, these trains (aka The PeopleMover) move at a speed of about seven miles per hour along almost a mile of track, beside or through many Tomorrowland attractions. They are operated by a linear induction motor that has no moving parts, uses little power, and emits no pollution.

The peaceful, breezy excursion lasts about 10 minutes. And there's rarely a line. It's one of our favorites.

**ASTRO ORBITER:** Here, passengers fly around for 1½ minutes in rockets designed to look more like Buck Rogers toys than 21st-century space shuttles. Riders are surrounded by vibrantly colored, whirling planets as they get an astronaut's-eye view of Tomorrowland.

**BIRNBAUM'S ★BEST★ SPACE MOUNTAIN:** 🎫 This crowd-pleaser first blasted onto the Magic Kingdom scene in 1975. In 2009, the classic attraction got a bit of a face-lift—and it immediately shot back to the top of thrill seekers' "must-do" lists. Rising to a height of more than 180 feet, the gleaming steel-and-concrete cone houses what most people call a roller coaster (Disney calls it a "roller-coaster-like" experience). The 2-minute, 30-second ride takes place in an outer-space-like darkness.

**Note:** Guests who are under 44 inches are not permitted to ride, and you must be in good health and free from heart conditions, motion sickness, back or neck problems, or other physical limitations to ride. Expectant mothers have to skip the trip. Children under 7 must be accompanied by an adult.

**TOMORROWLAND SPEEDWAY:** Little cars that burn up the tracks at this attraction provide quite a bit of the background noise in Tomorrowland. Kids especially enjoy the not-so-speedy, herky-jerky driving experience. The vehicles have rack-and-pinion steering and disc brakes, but unlike most cars, they run along a track. Yet, even expert drivers have trouble keeping them going in a straight line. (Don't panic when you notice the lack of a brake pedal—when you take your foot off the gas, the car comes to a quick halt.) The one-lap tour of Tomorrowland takes about 5 minutes.

**Note:** The minimum height requirement *to drive* is 54 inches. There is a 32-inch height requirement to ride shotgun. Babies younger than 12 months may not ride.

**WALT DISNEY'S CAROUSEL OF PROGRESS:** First seen at New York's 1964–65 World's Fair and moved here in 1975, this 21-minute experience showcases the evolution of the American family and how life changed —and ostensibly progressed—with the advent of electricity. The hook here is that as a scene ends, the audience moves to the next one—not unlike being on a carousel (hence the name of the attraction). This is a great place to escape the crowds and heat, not to mention take a much needed load off weary feet.

# Entertainment

In this most magical corner of the World, a tempting slate of live performances ranks among the more serendipitous discoveries. The Magic Kingdom's entertainment mix includes dazzling high-tech shows and old-fashioned numbers alike. To keep apprised of the offerings

on any given day, take a peek at a Times Guide.

While specifics are subject to change, the following is a good indication of the Magic Kingdom's repertoire.

### CAPTAIN JACK SPARROW'S PIRATE TUTORIAL:
So you wanna be a pirate? Who doesn't these days?! It just so happens, Captain Jack and his mate Mack are looking for new recruits near the Pirates of the Caribbean in Adventureland. They'd like to test your pirate skills (swordplay, menacing looks, etc.) and decide whether you're worthy of the Pirate's Oath and the title of honorary buccaneer.

### CASEY'S CORNER PIANO:
A pianist tickles the ivories of a snow-white upright daily at Casey's Corner restaurant on Main Street.

### DAPPER DANS:
You just might encounter a barber-shop quartet while strolling down Main Street, U.S.A. Conspicuously clad in straw hats and striped vests, the ever-so-jovial Dapper Dans tap-dance and let one-liners fly during their short four-part-harmony performances.

### CELEBRATE A DREAM COME TRUE PARADE:
A celebration of Disney animation, this 20-minute character-driven processional winds its way down Main Street once a day (in the afternoon).

### DREAM ALONG WITH MICKEY:
There's a dream-inspired party being thrown in front of Cinderella Castle—and just about everyone is invited. Mickey,

Minnie, Donald, and oodles of other Disney characters join the festivities as their dreams of adventure and "happily ever after" come to life through music and dance. (Though the evil Maleficent does try to spoil the fun, her efforts are thwarted.) The 20-minute show is presented on select days.

**BIRNBAUM'S ★BEST★ FIREWORKS:** "Wishes," a dynamite, pyrotechnic extravaganza, is presented most nights when the Magic Kingdom stays open after dark. Narrated by Jiminy Cricket, this is one of the biggest, boldest, and most eye-popping fireworks shows ever presented here. Showtime varies. Wishes is ideally viewed from Main Street, U.S.A., but can be seen from many vantage points. It is usually presented rain or shine.

**FLAG RETREAT:** At about 5 P.M. each day, patriotic music fills the air as a color guard marches to Town Square, in Main Street, U.S.A., and takes down the American flag that flies from the flagpole.

**MOVE IT, SHAKE IT, CELEBRATE IT! STREET PARTY:** An energetic street spectacle (Main Street, that is), this interactive show features a cast of characters, stilt walkers, and other performers—many of whom pop out of oversize gift boxes. Surprise! The 12- to 15-minute party is presented several times a day.

**BIRNBAUM'S ★BEST★ SPECTROMAGIC:** This dazzling display featuring more than 600,000 twinkling lights and character-laden floats winds through the Magic Kingdom during peak seasons and select evenings throughout the year. It's popular, so plan to stake out your viewing  spot about 45 minutes (or more) ahead of time.

**STORYTIME WITH BELLE:** In Fairytale Garden near Cinderella Castle, Belle invites young friends to help act out the story of Beauty and the Beast.

# Hot Tips

- Start the day by picking up a Fastpass assignment for your favorite attraction.

- If the weather's steamy, dress toddlers in waterproof diapers. Then they'll be free to frolic in the fountains in Fantasyland and Mickey's Toontown Fair.

- If there are two performances of the evening parade, the later one tends to draw smaller crowds.

- If you're driving to the park, start out very early. Most people tend to arrive between 9:30 A.M. and 11:30 A.M., and the roads and parking lots are jammed. Plan to be at the gates to the Magic Kingdom before they open, and then be on Main Street when the rest of the park opens.

- Certain attractions keep shorter hours than the park itself. To make sure you catch all your favorites, check a Times Guide.

- Dying to meet Mickey Mouse? Head for the Judge's Tent in Mickey's Toontown Fair. He greets visitors all day, every day. (The line tends to be shorter late in the day and during parades.)

- You can usually get in line for an attraction right up until the minute the park closes.

- Avoid the mealtime rush hours by eating early or late: before 11:30 A.M. or after 2 P.M., and before 5 P.M. or after 8 P.M.

- At busy times, take in these less-packed attractions: Walt Disney World Railroad, Liberty Belle Riverboat, Hall of Presidents, Country Bear Jamboree, and Tomorrowland Transit Authority.

- Check the Tip Board for information on the wait times for popular attractions.

- Break up your day. Consider heading back to your hotel (if it's not too far) for some swimming. Be sure to hold on to your admission pass, stroller and/or wheelchair receipt(s), and your parking stub, so that you can re-enter the Magic Kingdom.

- If an attraction has two lines, the one on the left usually will be shorter.

- There are picnic facilities at the Transportation and Ticket Center (TTC).

- Park guests have the right to chicken out at any time while waiting in line. Simply inform an attendant and you'll be discreetly whisked out a special exit.

- If you've rented a stroller, consider returning it just before the night's fireworks presentation. That way, after the show, you'll be able to make a beeline for your bed rather than stand in a line to return your stroller.

- Merchandise found in many shops at Walt Disney World is also available through mail order. Call 407-363-6200 for info.

- Travel light. The fewer bags, the faster you'll get through security.

- Allow extra time to get into the park—security and the "ticket tag" system can make for big delays—especially during peak times and "Extra Magic Hours."

- If your party decides to split up, set a meeting place and time. Avoid meeting in front of Cinderella Castle, since this area can become quite congested.

- Guests staying at the Contemporary resort can walk to and from the Magic Kingdom's front gate.

- Many Fantasyland attractions have dark moments and effects that may be too intense for timid toddlers.

- To up your score at Buzz Lightyear's Space Ranger Spin, always keep the trigger depressed. And aim for moving or faraway targets—they yield the most points.

# Magic Kingdom

## Hidden Mickeys*

Disney Imagineers have hidden Mickey's image all over Walt Disney World. Some are easier to track down than others. Here are some of the most popular "Hidden Mickeys" at the Magic Kingdom. How many can you find? Check the box when you spot each one!

❤ **Pirates of the Caribbean:** As you enter the main building, the line will split—take the left queue and keep your eyes peeled for four large gun cabinets hanging on both sides of the wall (you'll pass a set of smaller ones on the right before reaching these). The locks on the cabinets form Hidden Mickeys. ❏

❤ **Splash Mountain:** About halfway through the ride and in the room with jumping water, look quickly to your right and find a turtle floating on its back on a small geyser. Now look just above and behind the turtle for one of the most creative Hidden Mickeys in the park: It's a bobber attached to a fishing line! There is a more obvious one in the clouds beside the riverboat in the "Zip-a-dee-doo-dah" room, after the big splash. ❏

❤ **Big Thunder Mountain Railroad:** At the very end of the ride and after the train slows, look to your right to find two sets of gear shifts laying on the ground. The second set forms a Hidden Mickey, although you may notice that the dimensions are not quite proportional (the "ears" are significantly smaller than the "head"). ❏

❤ **The Haunted Mansion:** In the ghostly party scene, look at the bottom left corner of the banquet table for a Hidden Mickey made of two saucers and a plate. ❏

❤ **Mickey's Country House:** When you first walk through the door into Mickey's house, look at the wall in front of you to find a set of keys. The black key farthest to the right is shaped like Mickey. ❏

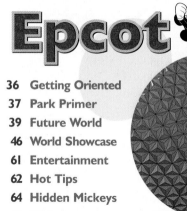

# Epcot

EPCOT

I magine a place whose entertainment inventory includes both a rich sampling of world cultures and a fun, enlightening journey to the technological frontier. You now have an inkling of the eye-opening and mind-broadening potential of Epcot—a place that's evolved most imaginatively in each of the 28 years it's been open.

The park consists of two areas of exploration: Future World and World Showcase. The former examines ideas in science and technology in ways that make them seem not only comprehensible but downright irresistible. The latter celebrates the diversity of the world's peoples, portraying a stunning array of nations with extraordinary devotion to detail.

A walkway from Future World leads to the World Showcase Promenade, a 1.2-mile thoroughfare that wraps around the lagoon, winding past each World Showcase pavilion in the process.

As you pass through Epcot's main Entrance Plaza, Spaceship Earth looms straight ahead. Pathways curve around the 180-foot-tall geosphere, winding up at Innoventions Plaza. Here, in addition to a show fountain, you'll see signs for Innoventions, whose two buildings cradle the east and west sides of the plaza. Beyond this central area, there are two roughly symmetrical north-south avenues; these are dotted with the six pavilions that form the outer perimeter of Future World. Mission: SPACE, Test Track, and Universe of Energy flank Spaceship Earth on the east, while Imagination!, The Land, and The Seas with Nemo & Friends lie to the west.

# Getting Oriented

Double the Magic Kingdom park and you have an idea of the size of Epcot. As for layout, the park is shaped something like a giant hourglass. Future World is anchored by the imposing silver "geosphere," dubbed Spaceship Earth. In World Showcase, the eleven international pavilions are arranged around the edge of World Showcase Lagoon.

## HOW TO GET THERE

**By car:** Take Exit 67 off I-4. Continue along to the Epcot Auto Plaza; if you park in a distant lot, take a tram to the park's main entrance.

**By WDW Transportation:** From the Grand Floridian, Contemporary, and Polynesian: hotel monorail to the Transportation and Ticket Center (TTC), then switch to the TTC-Epcot monorail. From the Magic Kingdom: express monorail to the TTC, then switch to the TTC-Epcot monorail. From Downtown Disney: bus to any resort, then transfer to an Epcot bus or boat. From Disney's Hollywood Studios, Animal Kingdom, all other Walt Disney World resorts, and the resorts on Hotel Plaza Boulevard: buses.

**Note:** A second Epcot park entrance, called International Gateway, provides entry directly to World Showcase. It may be reached via walkways and the *FriendShip* water launches from Disney's Hollywood Studios, plus the Swan, Dolphin, Yacht and Beach Club, and BoardWalk resorts. The boat deposits guests between the France and United Kingdom pavilions. It is possible to purchase admission here, at Epcot's "back door."

## PARKING

All-day parking at Epcot is $12 for day visitors (free to Disney resort guests with a resort ID, as well as annual passholders). Trams circulate regularly, providing transportation between the distant lots and the main entrance. Be sure to note the section and aisle in which you park. Parking tickets allow for re-entry to the area (and the other theme parks) throughout the day.

# Park Primer

## BABY FACILITIES

There are changing tables and facilities for nursing mothers at the Baby Care Center in the Odyssey Center, between Test Track and Mexico. Disposable diapers are kept behind the counter at many Epcot shops; just ask.

## CAMERA NEEDS

The Camera Center in Entrance Plaza and World Traveler at International Gateway stock memory cards, film, batteries, and disposable cameras. Stop at the Camera Center or at ImageWorks in Imagination! to transfer images from media cards to a CD.

## DISABILITY INFORMATION

Nearly all attractions, shops, and restaurants are accessible to guests using wheelchairs. Parking for guests with disabilities is available. Additional services are available for guests with visual and hearing disabilities. The *Guide for Guests with Disabilities* is available at Guest Relations. It provides a detailed overview of all services.

## FIRST AID

Minor medical problems can be handled at the First Aid Center, in the Odyssey Center, between Test Track and Mexico. Keep in mind that many guests could avoid a trip to First Aid simply by staying well hydrated. If you have an emergency, notify an employee.

## GETTING AROUND

Water taxis, called *FriendShip* launches, ferry guests across the World Showcase Lagoon. Docks are located near Mexico, Canada, Germany, and Morocco. (The only other way to traverse the vast area is on foot.)

## INFORMATION

Guest Relations, near Spaceship Earth, offers guide-maps, Times Guides, and a helpful staff.

## LOCKERS

Lockers are found beside Spaceship Earth. Cost is about $7, plus a $5 refundable deposit, for use all day.

## LOST & FOUND

Lost and Found is at Guest Relations on the east side of Spaceship Earth. After your visit, call 407-824-4245. If you find an item, present it to a park employee.

## LOST CHILDREN

Report lost children at Guest Relations or the Baby Care Center, and alert an employee.

## MONEY MATTERS

There are two ATMs in the park. Some foreign currency may be exchanged at Guest Relations. Credit cards (American Express, JCB, Discover, Diner's Club, Visa, MasterCard, Disney gift cards, and the Disney Visa Card), traveler's checks, Disney Dollars, and WDW resort IDs are accepted for admission and merchandise, as well as meals at most restaurants.

## PACKAGE PICKUP

Epcot shops can arrange for most purchases to be transported (for free) to the Gift Stop in Entrance Plaza or International Gateway for later pickup.

## SAME-DAY RE-ENTRY

Be sure to retain your ticket if you plan to return later the same day. A hand stamp is no longer required.

## SECURITY CHECK

Guests entering Disney theme parks will be subject to a security check. Backpacks, parcels, purses, etc. will be searched by security personnel before guests are permitted to enter.

## STROLLERS & WHEELCHAIRS

Strollers, wheelchairs, and Electric Convenience Vehicles (ECVs) may be rented at both park entrances. Wheelchairs are also available at the Gift Stop. A "Length-of-Stay" stroller rental yields a discount. Quantities are limited. ECVs tend to sell out early. Keep your rental receipt; it can be used that same day to get a replacement at Epcot or another theme park.

## TIP BOARDS

Check the digital boards in Innoventions Plaza and near Test Track throughout the day to learn current waiting times for the most popular attractions.

# Future World

A mere listing of the basic themes covered by the pavilions at Future World—agriculture, communications, car safety, the ocean, energy, imagination, and space—tends to sound a tad academic. But when these serious topics are presented with a special flair, they become part of an experience that ranks among Disney's most entertaining.

## Spaceship Earth

As it looms impressively just above the Earth, this great faceted silver structure looks a little bit like a spaceship ready to blast off. The recently "refreshed" show inside, which explores the continuing quest by human

beings to create the future, remains one of Epcot's compelling—if slower moving—attractions. It's an intriguing, narrated journey through time. It's also got an interactive element—it's simple, but everyone seems to get a kick out of it.

All of these sights are enough to keep heads turning as the "time machines" wend their way upward. The most dazzling scene is saved for the ride's finale, when the audience is placed in the heart of a communications revolution amid interactive global networks that tie all the peoples of the world together.

The Project Tomorrow post-show features five interactive areas, all emphasizing technology and its influence on daily life.

## Innoventions

A 100,000 square foot, forward-thinking showplace, Innoventions encourages guests to experience futuristic technologies today. It's an opportunity to test products that may soon change the way we live and work. Count on spending time exploring the exhibit areas (at least an hour). There's so much to see and do that curiosity will often get the better of any schedule here.

# The Seas with Nemo & Friends

Welcome to one of the largest facilities ever dedicated to humanity's relationship with the ocean. It was designed by Disney Imagineers, along with oceanographic experts and scientists. Inside, you'll find:

**TURTLE TALK WITH CRUSH:** If ever there was an attraction that left guests smiling and asking, "How do they do that?!"—this is it. The concept is simple enough—a 10-minute, animated show featuring the surfer-dude sea turtle from *Finding Nemo*. The amazing part? The cartoon critter interacts with the audience. In doing so, he imparts turtle-y wisdom, answers questions, and cracks a few jokes. It's like, totally awesome, dude. (There is usually a wait, so plan ahead.)

**THE SEAS WITH NEMO & FRIENDS ATTRACTION:** Imagineered in the style of classic family attractions, this undersea adventure is fun for all ages. In it, guests climb aboard a "clam-mobile" and enter a colorful coral reef. It seems Nemo has wandered off again and his teacher, Mr. Ray, needs help finding him. There's a bit of suspense involved—including moments of darkness and a jellyfish encounter—but rest assured, it all ends happily.

**CARIBBEAN CORAL REEF:** The man-made reef exists in an enormous tank that holds about six million gallons of water and more than 60 species of sea life. Among the 2,000 or so inhabitants are turtles, dolphins, and sharks. It's worth it to stop by as the park opens—that's usually when breakfast is served to the fish.

EPCOT

40

# The Land

Occupying six acres, this skylit pavilion gives guests a chance to soar above the clouds in a celebration of flight. A film, *The Circle of Life*, delivers an inspirational message about humanity and the environment. A boat ride explores farming in the past and future.

**LIVING WITH THE LAND:** 🅵🅿 The 13½-minute boat ride through the rainforest and greenhouses in this pavilion opens with a dramatic storm scene. Guests sail through rainforests, prairie grain fields, and a family farm. Recorded narration offers commentary on humans' struggle to cultivate and live in harmony with the land. Also of interest are the experiments being conducted to explore the practice of farming fish, and a desert farm area, where plants get nutrients through a drip irrigation system that delivers just the right amount of water. Quite fascinating, really.

**BIRNBAUM'S**
**★BEST★**

**SOARIN':** 🅵🅿 Up, up, and away! On this high-flying Epcot attraction, you'll be suspended in a hang glider 45 feet in the air, above a giant IMAX projection dome, and treated to an aerial tour of some of the most awe-inspiring landscapes the state of California has to offer.

With the wind in your hair and your legs dangling in the breeze, the multi-passenger hang glider feels so real that you may be tempted to pull up your feet for fear of hitting a treetop as you dip toward the ground.

In all, the airborne trip takes about 5 minutes and employs synchronized wind currents, scent machines, and a moving musical score set to a film that wraps 180 degrees around you, making this a thoroughly enveloping experience.

**Note:** You must be 40 inches tall and free of back problems, heart conditions, motion sickness, and other physical limitations to ride. The sensation of flight is quite realistic. If you're afraid of heights, sit this one out. And get your Fastpass as early as possible—they often run out by lunchtime.

**THE CIRCLE OF LIFE:** This 20-minute film uses animation and live action to illustrate some of the dangers to our environment, as well as potential solutions. Presented as a fable featuring *The Lion King* favorites Simba, Timon, and Pumbaa, the film takes an optimistic approach to a serious subject. It is shown in the Harvest Theater, just inside the entrance to The Land.

## Imagination!

With the lofty goal of sparking imagination in all of us, this pavilion provides some of the more whimsical experiences at Epcot. Among them:

### JOURNEY INTO IMAGINATION WITH FIGMENT:

Heeere's Figment! The beloved purple dragon is on hand to guide guests on a curious quest. The ambitious goal? To figure out the best way to capture your imagination.

The journey takes place at the Imagination Institute. It's a rather low-key experience, save for the occasional blast of air or flashing lights.

Nostalgia buffs, take note: The classic song "One Little Spark," which made its debut with the original version of this attraction, underscores the show once more.

### IMAGEWORKS: "WHAT IF" LABS: A true highlight

for youngsters is an area called Stepping Tones. It's hopscotch with a musical twist. One area of this playground encourages guests to morph pictures of themselves into flowers, puppies, and cartoon characters. Another attraction invites guests to wave their arms conductor-style and, by doing so, trigger a cacophony of sounds, some more melodious than others. Plan to spend at least a half hour exploring the area (especially if you've got young kids).

### HONEY, I SHRUNK THE AUDIENCE: FP

Welcome to the Imagination Institute, workplace of Professor Wayne Szalinski, the lead character in *Honey, I Shrunk the Kids* (the movie in which a scientist accidentally reduces his offspring to the size of ants).

This time, it's not just the kids who get shrunk—it's

the whole audience! Okay, it may be an illusion—thanks to a 3-D movie and some "4-D" effects—but it's pretty convincing.

**Note:** The effects in this 18-minute attraction give some guests the heebie-jeebies, especially those afraid of snakes or mice. If you suspect that you or any of your kids will have an adverse reaction, consider skipping the movie and heading to ImageWorks while the rest of your party watches the show.

BIRNBAUM'S ★BEST★ ## Test Track FP

Fasten your safety belt. This industrial-looking pavilion puts guests through the frenetic motions of automobile testing. As vehicles progress along the track, they whiz down straight-aways, hug hairpin turns, and face near-collisions—and not always in ideal road conditions. En route, riders learn how tests are performed in real facilities (called proving grounds) and discover why certain procedures are crucial to car safety.

The 5-minute ride begins with an uphill acceleration test. Then the suspension gets a workout, as vehicles descend over a bumpy surface that puts the wheels at odds with one another. During environmental testing, riders feel the heat and get the shivers as vehicles pass first through a radiant heat chamber, then a cold chamber. The ride takes a dramatic

(and exciting) turn during the road-handling segment. Finally, a long straightaway feeds into a series of banked turns and another straight shot that sends vehicles rocketing around the pavilion at top speed (up to 65 miles per hour).

**Note:** Kids under 7 must be accompanied by an adult; guests under 40 inches cannot ride; passengers must be free of back problems, heart conditions, motion sickness, and other physical limitations. Pregnant women must sit this one out.

## Mission: SPACE FP

Think you've got "the right stuff"? Well, this is your
chance to prove it. Epcot's out-of-this-world attraction
has a bold mission—to give you a chance to feel the
excitement and extreme intensity of space travel without ever leaving the planet.

There are actually two ways to travel to Mars at this
attraction: the original, "intense" way and the "less
intense" experience. Both versions of the Mission:
SPACE attraction provide a galaxy of thrills. The adventure begins with a white-knuckle blast-off of a spacecraft
(which has rather snug seating for four) on an important
mission to Mars. The sustained G-force during the
launch of the "highly intense" version is intended to be
most realistic. Once en route, expect a rather strange,
spectacular sensation. It's not quite weightlessness, but
according to astronauts who've felt the real thing, it's
pretty close. (So much so that it also tends to duplicate
the not-so-spectacular sensation of space sickness. In
fact, Mission: SPACE has the dubious distinction of
being the first attraction in theme park history to be
equipped with motion-sickness bags.)

Throughout the journey, you're expected to work
with your fellow crew members to accomplish the
mission. For the "intense" version, we recommend
ignoring this call to duty and keeping your eyes glued
to the screen. This will downsize the dizziness factor
and cut the chances of losing your lunch. You may be
tempted to tilt your head or shut your eyes. Don't.
(You will arrive on Mars whether you fulfill your
astronaut duty or not.)

Bottom line? Guests who don't get queasy on the

highly intense version tend to rave about Mission: SPACE. For us, well, we choose the alternative, gentler version of this ride. It's intended for those who would rather not take the risk. The experience is a bit different (there is no spinning, so no G-force), but it gives everyone a chance to ride without turning green.

**Note:** To ride either version, guests must be at least 44 inches tall and free of back and heart problems, motion sickness, and other physical limitations. Pregnant women must skip the trip, as should anyone with claustrophobic tendencies. And please don't eat anything before riding.

## BIRNBAUM'S **★BEST★** Universe of Energy

In the mood for a chuckle? Set a course for this attraction. You'll get a few giggles and learn something to boot.

Although it's easy to spot this pavilion's mirrored pyramid, the facade does not provide any clue at all to the 45 minutes of surprises in store. One of the most technologically complex experiences at Epcot, a show called Ellen's Energy Adventure consists of several movies and a ride-through segment.

The show begins with a film (featuring familiar faces). In it, Ellen is watching *Jeopardy!* One of the contestants is Ellen's annoying college roommate, Judy.

Ellen plays along but keeps striking out, particularly in the ENERGY category. As she watches, her neighbor Bill Nye, the Science Guy, pops in and is aghast at Ellen's ignorance. Shortly thereafter, Ellen dozes off. Ellen dreams she is a contestant on the show—and all of the questions are about energy!

The second segment leads guests into a theater, where Bill Nye vows to educate Ellen about the importance of energy. He persuades her to travel back in time to see where some of our energy sources came from. Suddenly (but very slowly), the whole seating area rotates, then breaks up into six sections that inch forward. The vehicles embark upon an odyssey through the primeval world. (The dinosaur zone may spook toddlers.)

The vehicles weigh about 30,000 pounds when loaded with passengers, yet are guided along the floor by a wire that is only *one-eighth inch thick*.

**Note:** At press time, this attraction was operating on a seasonal basis (as in "peak" times of year). Visit *www.disneyworld.com* for updates.

# World Showcase

Noble sentiments about humanity and the fellowship of nations, which have motivated so many World's Fairs in the past, also inhabit World Showcase. But make no mistake about it: This area of Epcot is unlike any previous international exposition.

The group of pavilions that encircles World Showcase Lagoon (a body of water with a perimeter of about 1.2 miles) demonstrates Disney conceptions about participating countries in remarkably realistic, consistently entertaining styles. You won't find the real Germany here—rather, the country's essence, much as a traveler returning from a visit might remember what he or she saw.

Shops, restaurants, and a handful of attractions are housed in a group of structures that is an artful pastiche of all the elements that give that nation's countryside and towns their distinctive flavor.

## Canada

Celebrating the many beauties of the U.S.A.'s neighbor to the north, the area devoted to the Western Hemisphere's largest nation is complete with its own mountain, waterfall, rushing stream, rocky canyon, mine, and splendid garden massed with colorful flowers. There's even a totem pole, a trading post, and an elaborate, mansard-roofed hotel similar to ones built by Canadian railroad companies as they pushed west around the turn of the 20th century. All this is imaginatively arranged somewhat like a split-level house, with the section representing French Canada on top, and another devoted to the mountains alongside it and below. From a distance, the Hôtel du Canada, the main building here, looks like little more than a bump on the land-scape—as does Epcot's single Canadian Rocky Mountain. But up close, they both seem to tower as high as the real thing.

The gardens were inspired by the Butchart Gardens, in Victoria, British Columbia, a famous park created on the site of a limestone quarry. The hotel is modeled, in part, after Ottawa's Victorian-style Château Laurier.

**O CANADA!:** This 18-minute motion picture (which was updated in 2008), presented in Circle-Vision 360, portrays the Canadian confederation in all its coast-to-coast splendor—the prairies and plains, sparkling shorelines and rivers, and the untouched snowfields and rocky mountainsides surround you.

**NORTHWEST MERCANTILE:** The first shop to the left upon entering the pavilion's plaza features Canadian-themed apparel such as nightshirts, aprons, T-shirts, and hockey jerseys. The shop also stocks plush toys, maple syrup, and other Canadian collectibles.

## United Kingdom

In the space of only a few hundred feet, visitors to this pavilion stroll from an elegant London square to the edge of a canal in the rural countryside—via a bustling urban English street framed by buildings that constitute a veritable rhapsody of historic architectural styles. But one scene leads to the next so smoothly that nothing ever seems amiss. Here again, note the attention to detail: the half-timbered High Street structure that leans a bit, the hand-painted "smoke" stains that make the chimneys look as if they have been there for centuries.

There's lots of entertainment, including a group of

comedians called the World Showcase Players—who, when not engaged in general clowning on the World Showcase Promenade, coax audience members into participating in their farcical playlets.

**THE CROWN & CREST:** This shop looks like a backdrop for a child's fantasy of the days of King Arthur, with its high rafters decked out with bright banners, vast fireplace (and crossed swords above), and wrought-iron chandelier. Name histories and family crests are available in addition to items for your personalized pub.

**SPORTSMAN SHOPPE:** Head here for clothing and accessories centered on uniquely British locales and sports. You can expect to find a selection of football (aka soccer) shirts and souvenirs.

**THE TEA CADDY:** Fitted out with heavy wooden beams and a broad fireplace to resemble the Stratford-upon-Avon cottage of William Shakespeare's wife, Anne Hathaway, this shop stocks English teas, both loose and in bags, in a wide variety of flavors. Other items include teapots, china, biscuits, and assorted candies and other treats.

**THE TOY SOLDIER:** This shop presents a nice variety of British toys, as well as a rather extensive selection of merchandise featuring that beloved gang from the Hundred Acre Wood: Winnie the Pooh, Piglet, Eeyore, and Tigger, too.

**THE QUEEN'S TABLE:** This shop (opposite the Sportsman Shoppe) is one of the loveliest in Epcot. This is particularly true of the store's Adams Room, embellished with elaborate moldings and a crystal chandelier, and painted in cream and robin's-egg blue.

**THE MAGIC OF WALES:** This small emporium offers rock 'n' roll memorabilia, highlighting British bands from the not-too-distant past.

## International Gateway

International Gateway, informally known as Epcot's back door, is located between the United Kingdom and France pavilions. Here, you can rent or get a replacement wheelchair or stroller, shop for souvenirs, or catch a *FriendShip* water taxi to the Yacht and Beach Club, BoardWalk, the Swan and Dolphin, and Disney's Hollywood Studios.

## France

The buildings here have mansard roofs and casement windows so Gallic in appearance that you may expect to see some sad Bohemian poet looking down from above. A canal-like offshoot of the lagoon seems like the Seine itself; the footbridge that spans it recalls the old Pont des Arts. There's a kiosk nearby like those that punctuate the streets of Paris, and a bakery whose heavenly aromas announce its presence long before it's visible. But most special of all are the people. Hosts and hostesses, who hail from Paris and the French provinces, answer questions in accented English.

Don't miss the garden on the opposite side of this arcade. It is one of Epcot's most peaceful spots.

**BIRNBAUM'S** **★BEST★** **IMPRESSIONS DE FRANCE:** Shown in the Palais du Cinéma, a little theater that's not unlike the one at Fontainebleau, this enchanting 18-minute film takes viewers on a trip through France.

The exceptionally wide screen adds yet another dimension. This is not a Circle-Vision 360 film like the movies shown at China and Canada. The France film used only five cameras, and it is shown on five large projection surfaces—200 degrees around. It's a beautiful film, one of the park's best. And the theater has seats!

**PLUME ET PALETTE:** This is one of the prettiest shops in World Showcase. The Art Nouveau style is reflected in the curves that embellish the wrought-iron balustrade edging the mezzanine and the moldings that decorate cherry-wood cabinets and shelves. Among the wares are purses and picture frames.

**LA SIGNATURE:** Another beautiful spot, this boutique features a selection of Guerlain cosmetics and fragrances.

**L'ESPRIT DE PROVENCE:** This little store stocks French textiles, ceramics, and kitchen accessories inspired by the Provence region in the south of France.

**LES VINS DE FRANCE:** Selections in this wine shop range from the inexpensive to the pricey, from *vin ordinaire* going for several dollars to upward of $99 for a rare vintage. Wine tastings are held here to sample the offerings (note that a charge is levied for each taste). Books and wine accessories are available, too.

**SOUVENIRS DE FRANCE:** Everything from Eiffel Tower statues to CDs with music by French composers are the stock-in-trade at this location near the exit of the cinema. Other potential souvenirs: berets, pins, thimbles, flags, coasters, and mouse pads. The area is based on Paris's now-demolished Les Halles, the city's old fruit and vegetable market.

## Morocco

Nine tons of tile were handmade, hand cut, and shipped to Epcot to create this World Showcase pavilion. To capture the unique quality of this North African country's architecture, Moroccan artisans came to Epcot to practice the mosaic art that has been a part of their homeland for thousands of years. Koutoubia Minaret, a detailed replica of the famous prayer tower in Marrakesh, stands guard at the entrance. A courtyard with a fountain at the center leads to the Medina (Old City). An ancient working waterwheel irrigates the gardens, and the motifs repeated throughout the buildings include carved plaster and wood, tile, and brass. Mo'Rockin takes over the courtyard, with musicians playing lively Western music with an Arabic twist. (Entertainment varies.)

**CASABLANCA CARPETS:** Featuring an impressive and eclectic inventory, this elegant emporium offers carpets, jewelry, lamps, books, and fezzes.

**MOROCCAN NATIONAL TOURIST OFFICE:** A center offering literature useful in planning a visit to Morocco, this is also the place to inquire about experiencing a "Morocco Tour." The guided tour of the pavilion includes a description of the culture, history, and architecture of Morocco. Tours are held daily. They are free and last from about 20 to 45 minutes.

**TANGIER TRADERS:** This is the place to shop if you're in the market for a fez, woven belts, leather sandals and purses, and other traditional Moroccan clothing and accessories.

**MARKETPLACE IN THE MEDINA:** Hand-woven baskets, sheepskin wallets and bags, assorted straw hats, drums, sandals, postcards, scarves, and small carpets are among the available items.

**THE BRASS BAZAAR:** Interspersed among the decorative brass plates in this store are ceramic pitchers, planters, pots, ornate bottles of rosewater, serving sets, soapstone carvings, wooden collectibles, books, framed prints, and other Moroccan wares.

**SOUK AL MAGREB:** This waterside enclave spills over with crafted brass work. Moroccan baskets and leather goods also abound. In addition to henna tattoos (applied by a resident tattoo artist), one can also pick up toy camels, hats, and shirts.

# Japan

Serenity rules in Japan. Except, of course, when the pavilion resounds with traditional music performed by a drum-playing duo or group.

The landscaping, designed in accordance with traditional symbolic and aesthetic values, contributes to the pavilion's peaceful mood. Rocks, which in Japan represent the enduring nature of the Earth, were brought from North Carolina and Georgia (since boulders are scarce in the Sunshine State). Water, symbolizing the sea (which the Japanese consider a life source), is abundant; the Japan pavilion garden has a stream and pools inhabited by *koi*

(carp). Evergreen trees, which in Japan are symbols of eternal life, are here in force.

The pagoda was modeled after an eighth-century structure located in the Horyuji Temple, in Nara, Japan. The striking *torii* gate on the shore of World Showcase Lagoon derives from the design of the one at the Itsukushima shrine in Hiroshima Bay.

**BIJUTSU-KAN GALLERY:** Housing a changing cultural display, this small museum has offered, among other exhibitions, "Netsuke—Historic Carvings of Old Japan," a showcase of traditional Japanese art forms, and, more recently, the Kitahara Collection of Tin Toys, featuring toys produced from 1880 to 1970.

**MITSUKOSHI MERCHANDISE STORE:** There are T-shirts bearing Japanese characters, traditional headdresses, and a selection of bowls and vases meant for flower arranging for sale at this spacious store set up by Mitsukoshi—a four-century-old retail firm.

The shop features a selection of kimonos and Hello Kitty paraphernalia, as well as chopsticks, bonsai, jewelry, china, paper fans, and origami products. There is also a bounty of snacks, candies, and tea.

# The American Adventure

When it came to creating The American Adventure, the centerpiece of World Showcase, Disney Imagineers were given relatively free rein. So the 110,000 bricks of the imposing Colonial-style structure that houses a spectacular show, restaurant, and souvenir shop are the real thing—patiently crafted *by hand* from soft Georgia clay.

The show inside stands out because of its evocative settings, its detailed sets, and the 35 Audio-Animatronics players, some of the most lifelike ever created by the Disney organization. A stellar a cappella vocal group called Voices of Liberty periodically serenades guests in the building's foyer. By all means, catch a performance.

**BIRNBAUM'S** **★BEST★** **THE AMERICAN ADVENTURE SHOW:** One of the outstanding Epcot attractions, this 26-minute presentation celebrates the American spirit from our nation's earliest years right up to the present. Beginning with the arrival of the Pilgrims at Plymouth Rock, the Audio-Animatronics narrators—a lifelike Ben Franklin and a convincing, cigar-puffing Mark Twain—recall key people and events in American history.

The idea is to recall episodes in history (positive and negative) that contributed to the growth of the spirit of America, by engendering "a new burst of creativity" or "a better understanding of ourselves as partners in the American experience."

Seats toward the front of the house give the best view of the Audio-Animatronics figures. The sound is better here, too. If you have some extra time before the show, be sure to read the inspirational quotes on the walls.

**AMERICAN HERITAGE GALLERY:** Located inside the American Adventure pavilion, the addition of this art gallery brought Epcot's grand total to six. Its current exhibition, which opened in late 2007, is called "National Treasures." Among the items that have been here to gaze upon? Thomas Edison's phonograph and baseball mementos that belonged to Jackie Robinson.

**HERITAGE MANOR GIFTS:** Visit this shop to find Americana in all of its red-white-and-blue glory. Gifts include clothing, flags, and books about U.S. history.

**AMERICA GARDENS THEATRE:** An ever-changing slate of entertainment is presented throughout the year in this lakeside amphitheater in front of the American Adventure pavilion. Showtimes are also posted on the promenade and in the Times Guide.

# Italy

The arches and cutout motifs that adorn the World Showcase reproduction of the Doge's Palace in Venice are the more obvious examples of the attention to detail lavished on the individual structures in this pavilion. The angel perched atop the scaled-down campanile was sculpted on the model of the original, right down to the curls on the back of its head. It was then covered with real gold leaf, despite the fact that it was destined to be set almost 100 feet in the air.

St. Mark the Evangelist is remembered, together with the lion that is the saint's companion and Venice's guardian; these can be seen atop the two massive columns that flank the small arched footbridge that connects the island to the mainland. The only deviation from Venetian reality is the alteration of the site of the Doge's Palace in reference to the real St. Mark's Square.

**ENOTECA CASTELLO:** This shop on the edge of the piazza features a selection of red and white Italian wines. Items such as chocolate, espresso, cookbooks, and decorative bottle toppers are also on hand.

**IL BEL CRISTALLO:** There is an abundance of fine leather goods, including purses, wallets, and bags, inside this shop. Other featured wares include scarves, ties, fragrances, and jewelry.

**LA BOTTEGA ITALIANA:** This shop sells an eclectic blend of decorative ceramics and glassware, plus hand-crafted Venetian masks and hand-crafted holiday ornaments made especially for Epcot guests.

# Germany

There are no villages in Germany quite like this one. Inspired by various towns in the Rhine region, Bavaria, and the German north, it boasts structures reminiscent of those found in urban enclaves as diverse as Frankfurt, Freiburg, and Rothenburg. There are stair-stepped rooflines and towers, balconies and arcaded walkways, and so much overall charm that the scene seems to come straight out of a fairy tale.

**DAS KAUFHAUS:** This two-story structure, whose exterior is patterned after a merchants' hall known as the Kaufhaus (found in the town of Freiburg im Breisgau, Germany), stocks glassware and housewares.

**VOLKSKUNST:** This establishment boasts a burgher's bounty of German timepieces, plus other items made by hand in the rural corners of the nation. As for cuckoo clocks, some are small and unobtrusive, whereas others are so immense that they'd look appropriate only in some cathedral-ceilinged hunting lodge. This is also the place to pick up a traditional German beer stein—there is a nice selection from which to choose. Unique, hand-painted eggs are also available. (They are painted in the shop by a German artist.)

**DER TEDDYBAR:** Located next to to Volkskunst (on the right side of the pavilion when facing it from World Showcase promenade), this toy shop would be a delight if only for the lively mechanized displays: Some of the stuffed lambs and the dolls wearing folk dresses (called *dirndls*) have been animated so that tails wag and skirts swirl in time to German folk tunes. The shop is also home to a selection of toys, including expensive stuffed keepsakes from Steiff. Last but not least, you can have dolls created to your personal specifications.

**KUNSTARBEIT IN KRISTALL:** This shop to the left of the Biergarten features Austrian crystal jewelry, tall beer mugs, wineglasses in traditional German tints of green and amber, and crystal decanters. Guests may have glassware etched on the spot.

**SUSSIGKEITEN:** It's a mistake to visit this tiny confectionery shop on an empty stomach: Chocolate cookies, butter cookies, and almond biscuits mix with caramels, fudge, nuts, and caramel apples, and there are boxes upon boxes of *lebkuchen*, the spicy, chewy cookies traditionally baked in Germany at Christmas.

**WEINKELLER:** The Germany pavilion's wine shop, situated toward the rear of St. Georgsplatz, offers about 50 varieties of German wine. Wine tastings are held here daily (for a price). The selection includes not only those vintages meant for everyday consumption, but also fine estate wines. These are white (with a few exceptions), because white wine constitutes the bulk of Germany's vinicultural output. The setting itself is attractive—low-ceilinged and cozy, and full of cabinets embellished with carvings of vines and grapes.

**DIE WEIHNACHTS ECKE:** This shop can set a visitor's mind to thoughts of Christmas even on the hottest dog days of summer. Ornaments, decorations, and gifts made by German companies line the shelves of this store. Among them are wood carvings made in the town of Oberammergau, nutcrackers, and "smokers" (carved wooden dolls with a receptacle for incense and a hollow pipe for the smoke to escape).

# China

Dominated by the Disney equivalent of Beijing's Temple of Heaven and announced by a pair of banners that proclaim good wishes to passersby (the Chinese

characters translate to: "May good fortune follow you on your path through life" and "May virtue be your neighbor"), this pavilion conveys a level of serenity that offers an appealing contrast to the hearty merriment of the bordering Germany and the gaiety of nearby Mexico. Live flute, zither, or dulcimer music is performed inside the Temple of Heaven, while agile acrobats do tricks in the courtyard. The gardens also make a major contribution. They are full of rosebushes native to China, and there is a century-old mulberry tree (to the left of the main walkway into the pavilion). Be sure to stand on the round stone in the center of the main structure: Every whisper is amplified.

**REFLECTIONS OF CHINA:** This presentation shows the beauties of a land that few Epcot visitors have seen firsthand.

Filmmakers used nine cameras to capture cultural and scenic images that will wrap completely around viewers. The tour includes stops in Hong Kong, Macau, Beijing, and Shanghai. It includes footage of many landmarks, such as the 2,400-year-old Great Wall and Tian'anmen Square, as well as some newer cultural developments. Overall, it showcases the majesty of this ancient country and highlights some of the changes that have taken place over the past decades. Note that the theater has no seats.

**HOUSE OF WHISPERING WILLOWS:** When exiting, pass by the House of Whispering Willows, an exhibit of ancient Chinese art and artifacts. Changed about every six months, it invariably includes fine pieces from well-known collections.

**YONG FENG SHANGDIAN:** This vast Chinese emporium offers a huge assortment of merchandise—silk robes, prints, embroidered items, and more. Trinkets, moderately priced items, and expensive antiques are available. The calligraphy on the curtains wishes passers-by good fortune, long life, prosperity, and happiness.

## Norway

Built in conjunction with many Norwegian companies, the pavilion celebrates the rich history, folklore, and culture of one of the Western world's oldest countries.

The cobblestone town square is an architectural showcase of the styles of such Norwegian towns as Bergen, Alesund, and Oslo. There's also a Norwegian castle fashioned after Akershus, a 14th-century fortress still standing in Oslo's harbor. Few can resist walking into the bakery for a taste of its treats. Shops stock handicrafts and folk items: hand-knit woolens, wood carvings, and glass and metal artwork.

For a free guided tour of the pavilion in addition to a crash course in Norwegian culture and architecture, stop by the Norway Tourism desk.

The main attraction here? An attraction that whisks guests away via Viking ship.

**MAELSTROM:** [FP] Visitors tour Norway by boat—16-passenger, dragon-headed longboats inspired by those Eric the Red and other Vikings used. The 5-minute voyage begins in a 10th-century Viking village. Seafarers soon find themselves in a mythical Norwegian forest, populated by trolls who send the boats through a maelstrom to the grandeur of the Geiranger fjord, where the vessel nearly spills over a waterfall.

Survivors disembark and enter a movie theater, where the journey continues on-screen for about five more minutes. If you wish to skip the flick, walk straight through the theater to exit.

**STAVE CHURCH GALLERY:** Inside the wooden stave church, there is an exhibit that explores Vikings and Norwegian culture. It's interesting (and sad) to note that only 30 stave churches remain in Norway today.

**THE PUFFIN'S ROOST:** Norwegian gifts, sweaters, activewear, fragrances, jewelry, Christmas items, candy, toys, and trolls are the wares here.

## Mexico

Dominated by a re-creation of a quaint plaza at dusk, the pyramid's interior is rimmed by balconied, tile-roofed, colonial-style structures. Crowding a pretty fountain area is a quartet of stands selling Mexican handicrafts. Take a

look at the cultural exhibit inside the pyramid entrance on the way in. Note that the building was inspired by Meso-American structures dating from the third century A.D. Of course, the biggest draw in these parts is the boat ride.

**GRAN FIESTA TOUR STARRING THE THREE CABALLEROS:** Big news! The Three Caballeros (that would be Donald Duck, José, and Panchito) are reuniting for a big show in Mexico City! Unfortunately, the ever-mischievous Donald has gone missing in Mexico—and guests join Panchito and José in the quest to find him. In doing so, you will be treated to a whirlwind (if slow-moving) boat tour of the country. The cheery montage of film, props, and Audio-Animatronics figures is reminiscent of It's a Small World, though on a much smaller scale.

**PLAZA DE LOS AMIGOS:** Even if you're not in a buying mood, make a point of stopping by to take a look at this bustling marketplace. Brightly colored paper flowers, sombreros, malachite, baskets, piñatas, mariachi music (available on CD), and pottery make this *mercado* (market) as bright and almost as lively as one in Mexico itself. Authentic pre-Columbian figures are on display. Also available for purchase are spices, liquors (emphasis on tequila), and musical instruments.

**EL RANCHITO DEL NORTE:** Located on the lagoon side of World Showcase Promenade, this spot features gifts and souvenirs.

**LA FAMILIA FASHIONS:** Traditional and modern Mexican accessories; the handcrafted silver jewelry is a major draw.

## Showcase Plaza

**PORT OF ENTRY:** A children's shop carrying infants' and kids' clothing, girls' character dresses, and toys.

**DISNEY TRADERS:** Merchandise combining the charms of classic Disney characters and World Showcase themes is the primary stock-in-trade. Sunglasses and sundries are also sold.

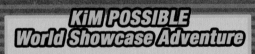

### KiM POSSIBLE World Showcase Adventure

Ready to release your inner secret agent and save the world from super-villains? Then this free, interactive quest (based on Disney Channel's *Kim Possible*) is for you. To sign up, head to a Team Possible recruitment center (at Innoventions or on the Odyssey Bridge). Once you get a "Kimmunicator" and mission assignment, you're good to go. Each of the 7 different missions was designed with groups in mind (two to four agents can share a Kimmunicator) and lasts about 45 to 60 minutes.

# Entertainment

Epcot presents an intriguing array of live performances each day, making it very important to consult a park Times Guide when you arrive.

**AMERICA GARDENS THEATRE:** The venue alongside the lagoon at The American Adventure pavilion hosts an ever-changing program of live entertainment. Check a Times Guide for current offerings.

**BIRNBAUM'S**
**★BEST★**

**ILLUMINATIONS—REFLECTIONS OF EARTH:** This nighttime spectacular presents the entire history of our planet in 13 minutes—from its creation to the present and a look toward the future. A dazzling mix of lasers, fireworks, fountains, and music, this show is a highlight of any Epcot visit.

The extravaganza, visible from anywhere on the World Showcase Promenade, takes place nightly at closing time. There are excellent viewing locations all around the World Showcase Lagoon, though it is generally most crowded on the Showcase Plaza side of the lake (due to its proximity to the park's main turnstiles).

**KIDCOT FUN STOPS:** There is an activity area in each of the countries of World Showcase and at Future World's The Seas with Nemo & Friends, Innoventions, and The Land. These spots allow young guests to play games and make crafts that are native to different cultures. The areas are best enjoyed by small children.

**WORLD SHOWCASE PERFORMERS:** It's all but impossible to complete a circuit of World Showcase without catching a few performances en route. Keep an eye on the schedule to take in live entertainment at each pavilion, often performed by natives of the country represented. Among the possibilities: worldly comedians, a Mexican mariachi band, Moroccan belly dancers, Chinese acrobats, a kilt-clad Canadian rock band (known as "Off-Kilter"), Japanese drummers, a mop-topped British quartet (called "The British Invasion"), African storytellers, and more.

# Hot Tips

- On your way into the park, pick up a complimentary guidemap and a Times Guide. Consult the entertainment schedule right away!

- Lines throughout Epcot are longest at midday and shortest in the early evening.

- If you have a reservation for a table-service restaurant, plan to arrive a few minutes ahead of time.

- Check the Tip Boards in Innoventions Plaza and on both sides of Future World for wait times at the most popular attractions and adjust your plans accordingly. And use Fastpass whenever possible.

- If you plan to play at ImageWorks, the play area inside Imagination!, take along the e-mail address of a friend. It may come in handy.

- Interactive, soft-surface fountain areas at Epcot provide guests of all ages with an opportunity to cool off. Be sure to pack swimsuits (and waterproof diapers) for little ones who will likely spend time splashing in the water.

- When it comes to park-hopping, Epcot is an ideal park to hop to. It's usually open late.

- Allow plenty of time to explore the hands-on exhibits at Innoventions East and West, and ImageWorks in the Imagination! pavilion.

- The line for Spaceship Earth is usually quite long in the morning and relatively short in the late afternoon or early evening.

- *FriendShip* water taxis are unlikely to transport you across World Showcase Lagoon any faster than a brisk walk, but they are a peaceful, foot-friendly way to make the half-mile-plus journey.

- Keep an eye (or ear) out for the talking water fountain near the Imagination! pavilion.

- Future World's Club Cool offers free samples of a variety of Coca-Cola soft drinks from around the world. (We think one is rather yucky, but the others are quite refreshing.)

- If you don't mind splitting up your party, head for the "single rider" line at Test Track. It moves a bit faster than the standby line.

- Future World usually opens earlier and closes earlier than World Showcase.

- World Showcase opens at 11 A.M., but guests may enter the park's front entrance or back door (aka International Gateway) up to a half hour prior to the opening of Future World.

- While all of the seats in the American Adventure theater provide good views, the sound quality is best in the middle and toward the front.

- Don't try to fit all three World Showcase movies into one day. They aren't going anywhere.

- The Wonders of Life pavilion is not expected to be open in 2010.

- If Spaceship Earth has failed to make your "must-see" list in the past, you may want to revisit "The Ball"—a "refresh" provided a spiffy look and added a few surprises.

# Epcot

## Hidden Mickeys*

These are some of the most popular "Hidden Mickeys" at Epcot. How many can you find? Check the box when you spot each one!

♥ **Soarin':** At the very end of the ride, as you soar into the sky over Disneyland, the second burst of fireworks forms a huge Hidden Mickey. ❏

♥ **Mission: SPACE:** After you exit the ride and enter the gift shop, look up in the center of the room to find a side profile of Mickey painted on the ceiling. ❏

♥ **Test Track:** At the very end of the entrance queue and just before you are assigned to a pre-show room, look at the demonstration labeled "7B Knee Calibration" on the left. Look for a desk and search for three washers (flat circular pieces of metal) that form an upside-down Mickey on the left edge. Next, find the shelves to the right of the desk and look at the top shelf for a red Mickey toy. ❏

♥ **American Adventure pavilion:** Look for a painting of early American settlers crossing a river with covered wagons. One of the wagon-pulling oxen has a Mickey near its left front leg. ❏

♥ **Norway pavilion:** In the stave church's Vikings exhibit, find King Olaf II and examine his tunic for a navy blue Hidden Mickey close to his right thigh. ❏

♥ **Morocco pavilion:** Next to the lagoon and just outside Morocco's main pavilion, you'll see a shop called Souk Al Magreb. One of the green doors to the shop has three brass plates toward the top that form a Hidden Mickey. ❏

♥ **France pavilion:** Locate the Librairie et Galerie (it's opposite the Guerlain shop, on the right side of the pavilion) and examine the books. On the top shelf, find the red rose and move to the right to find a Hidden Mickey worn into the binding of a book. ❏

♥ **The Seas with Nemo & Friends:** In Bruce's Shark World, look for two large posters—one titled "Did You Know?" and the other titled "Bruce's Scrapbook" (they are on opposite sides of the room). Each has an oyster in the lower right corner that contains Mickey-shaped pearls. ❏

♥ **Journey Into Imagination with Figment:** About halfway through the ride and as you move through Figment's house, look up in the bathroom. Figment's toilet forms a Hidden Mickey with two red circles on the ground next to it. ❏

♥ **Spaceship Earth:** In the Renaissance scene, look quickly to your left to find the first painter standing in front of a table (his back is to you). On the top left of the table, three white-paint circles form a Hidden Mickey. Later in the ride, keep your eyes open for a Hidden "WDI" (the abbreviation for Walt Disney Imagineering) on the microphone of the radio broad-caster (on your left). ❏

♥ **Living with the Land:** As you walk through the queue, try to find the three bubbles on the large mural that come together to form a Hidden Mickey. (Hint: It's near the middle of the mural.) ❏

*\* Specifics may change during 2010.*

# Epcot Dining

Should you find yourself without reservations to a table-service spot, grab a bite at one of the many quick-service establishments. The list* of such eateries includes the following:

**BOULANGERIE PATISSERIE:** Epcot veterans are on to something here. Their perennial favorite never fails to deliver. In addition to the pastries, a small but enticing selection of snacks is offered (think quiche, baguettes, and ham and cheese croissants).

**ELECTRIC UMBRELLA:** Desperate for something healthy? Look no further than this spot's whole wheat veggie wrap. Also on the menu are cheeseburgers, chicken salad, grilled chicken sandwiches, and chicken nuggets.

**KRINGLA BAKERI OG KAFE:** Tucked inside the Norway pavilion, this shop sells *kringles* and sweet pretzels, not to mention strawberry cheesecake and Norwegian school bread.

**SOMMERFEST:** Bratwurst sandwiches and hot dogs are the staples here. Soft pretzels, Black Forest cake, apple strudel, and cheesecake are also on the menu.

**SUNSHINE SEASONS:** One-stop shopping is at the ready. This cluster of windows comprises an honest-to-goodness food court that is a cut above the norm. It's crazy busy during mealtimes, so try to go a little before or after the traditional lunch or dinner bell rings.

**YAKITORI HOUSE:** Okay, so the selection is limited. It's still pretty rewarding to get a bit of sushi on the fly. Other options include teriyaki chicken, sukiyaki beef, and Japanese sweets.

**YORKSHIRE COUNTY FISH SHOP:** Fabulous fish and chips. 'Nuf said.

* Note that, while all of the above participate in the Disney Dining Plan, only Sunshine Seasons offers breakfast selections.

# Disney's Hollywood Studios

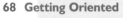

**DISNEY'S HOLLYWOOD STUDIOS**

**D**isney's Hollywood Studios (formerly known as Disney-MGM Studios) has been described as "the Hollywood that never was and always will be." A bit hokey, perhaps—but also true. Enter the gates and the mosaic of flashy neon, chromed Art Deco, streamlined architecture, and star-gazing street characters immediately plunges you into the Hollywood of the 1940s. A nostalgic view of the movie-making capital has been combined with backstage tours and a variety of TV- and movie-themed attractions.

The Studios' water tower, known to punsters (for obvious reasons) as the "Earful Tower," is reminiscent of the structures looming over Hollywood studios of the Golden Age. Here, however, it gets that special Disney touch—it's capped by a Mouseketeer-style hat. In true Hollywood style, this established star has been somewhat upstaged by the most unlikely of attention grabbers: a towering Sorcerer Mickey hat, stationed at the far end of Hollywood Boulevard.

Since opening in 1989, the park continues to expand and evolve. Its eclectic lineup of classic attractions is joined by such thrillers as: the always scary Tower of Terror, the rollicking Rock 'n' Roller Coaster, a dynamic vehicle stunt show, and an explosive struggle between good and evil in Fantasmic! Each adds a whole new dimension to the Hollywood term *action*.

# Getting Oriented

While Disney's Hollywood Studios is much smaller than Epcot, the park has a sprawling layout with no distinctive shape or main thoroughfare. As such, the Studios can be a bit of a challenge to navigate. Be sure to study a guidemap as you enter.

The park entrance is at Hollywood Boulevard. This shop-lined avenue leads straight to Hollywood Plaza, address of the Studios' Chinese Theater, a replica of Grauman's Theatre that doubles as the site of The Great Movie Ride (it's hidden behind the giant Sorcerer Mickey hat). Walking along Hollywood Boulevard toward the plaza, you'll come to Hollywood Junction. Here, a wide, palm-fringed thoroughfare known as Sunset Boulevard branches off to the right.

Stroll down Sunset Boulevard and you will come across The Hollywood Hills amphitheater, home of Fantasmic, and Rock 'n' Roller Coaster. At the street's far end is the Hollywood Tower Hotel, home of The Twilight Zone™ Tower of Terror. The strip is also graced with shops, the Sunset Ranch Market, and the Theater of the Stars amphitheater, where Beauty and the Beast—Live on Stage is performed daily.

Stand in Hollywood Plaza, facing the Sorcerer Hat, and you'll notice an archway just off to your right. This leads to Animation Courtyard. Pixar Place, the area on the street veering off to the left of Animation Courtyard, leads to Toy Story Mania and the Studio Backlot Tour. If you turn left off Hollywood Boulevard and go past Echo Lake, you're on course for such attractions as Sounds Dangerous Starring Drew Carey, Indiana Jones Epic Stunt Spectacular, and Star Tours. Just beyond Star Tours, there is another entertainment zone, near the Streets of America (in the backlot area). The biggies to see here: Muppet*Vision 3-D and Lights, Motors, Action— Extreme Stunt Show. Little ones enjoy the Honey, I Shrunk the Kids Movie Set Adventure.

## HOW TO GET THERE

**By car:** Take Exit 64B off I-4. Continue about half a mile to reach the parking area. Take a tram to the park entrance.

**By WDW Transportation:** From the Swan, Dolphin, Yacht and Beach Club, and BoardWalk: boat or walkway. From Fort Wilderness: bus from the Settlement stop. From the Magic Kingdom: ferry or monorail to the Ticket and Transportation Center, then bus to the Studios. From Epcot, Animal Kingdom, all other Walt Disney World resorts, and the resorts on Hotel Plaza Boulevard: bus. From Downtown Disney: bus to any Walt Disney World resort and transfer to a Studios bus or boat.

## PARKING

All-day parking at the Studios is $12 for day visitors (free to WDW resort guests and annual passholders). Trams circulate regularly, providing transportation from the parking area to the park entrance. Be sure to note the section and the aisle in which you park. The parking ticket you receive allows for re-entry to the parking area throughout the day.

## HOURS

Disney's Hollywood Studios is usually open from 9 A.M. until about sunset. During certain holiday periods and summer months, hours are extended. It's best to arrive about 20 minutes before the posted opening time—guests are often let in early. Depending on the season, some stage shows do not open until late in the morning.

# Park Primer

## BABY FACILITIES

Changing tables and facilities for nursing mothers can be found at the Baby Care Center at Guest Relations near the park entrance.

## CAMERA NEEDS

The Darkroom on Hollywood Boulevard stocks memory cards, batteries, film, and disposable cameras.

## DISABILITY INFORMATION

Most attractions, restaurants, shops, and shows are accessible to guests using wheelchairs. Additional services are available for guests with visual or hearing disabilities. For a detailed overview of the services offered, including transportation, parking, attraction access, and more, pick up a copy of the *Guide for Guests with Disabilities* at Guest Relations.

## FIRST AID

Minor medical problems can be handled at the First Aid Center, located next to Guest Relations at the park entrance.

## INFORMATION

Guest Relations, located just inside the park entrance, has free guidemaps and Times Guides and an ever-resourceful staff. To make same-day dining arrangements for certain Studios eateries, head over to the booth at the junction of Hollywood and Sunset boulevards.

## LOCKERS

Lockers can be found by Oscar's Super Service, near the entrance. They may be rented from the Crossroads of the World kiosk, directly across from Oscar's classic pickup truck. Your receipt entitles you to a locker at any other theme park on the same day (not including the deposit).

## LOST & FOUND

Located near the park entrance, past the turnstiles on the right. To report lost items after your visit, call 407-824-4245.

## LOST CHILDREN

Report lost children at Guest Relations, or alert a Disney employee to the problem.

## MONEY MATTERS

There are two ATMs at this park. In addition to cash, credit cards (American Express, Visa, Discover, Disney Visa, JCB, Diner's Club, and Master Card), traveler's checks, Disney gift cards, and Walt Disney World resort IDs are accepted for admission, merchandise, and meals at all restaurants. Some snack carts and souvenir stands may accept cash only.

## PACKAGE PICKUP

Shops can arrange for purchases to be transported to package pickup at the Lost and Found, where they can be picked up later. The service is free. Walt Disney World resort guests may have items sent to their respective resorts at no charge.

## SAME-DAY RE-ENTRY

Be sure to retain your ticket if you plan to return later the same day. A hand-stamp is no longer required for re-entry.

## SECURITY CHECK

Guests entering Disney theme parks will be subject to a security check. Bags will be searched by Disney security personnel before guests are permitted to enter the park.

## STROLLERS & WHEELCHAIRS

Strollers, double strollers, wheelchairs, and Electric Convenience Vehicles (ECVs) may be rented from Oscar's Super Service, inside the park entrance on the right. A "Length of Stay" rental ticket saves renters a bit off the daily cost. Anything rented at the Studios must stay at the Studios. Keep the receipt—it can be used on the same day for a replacement at any theme park. Quantities are limited.

## TIP BOARD

Check the Tip Boards at the junction of Hollywood and Sunset boulevards and on the Streets of America to learn the wait times for the most popular attractions in the park. Attendants can answer questions, too.

# The Main Attractions

## The Twilight Zone™ Tower of Terror [FP]

**BIRNBAUM'S**
**★BEST★** The Hollywood Tower Hotel is the creepy home of a spectacular thrill ride. On the facade of the 199-foot-tall building hangs a sparking electric sign. As the legend goes, lightning struck the building on Halloween night in 1939. An entire guest wing disappeared, along with an elevator carrying five people.

The line for the ride runs through the lobby, where dusty furniture and cobwebs add to the eerie atmosphere. Guests are led to the boiler room to enter the ride elevator. (If you change your mind about riding, simply ask the attendant to direct you toward the "chicken exit.") Once you take a seat in the elevator, the doors close and the room begins its ascent. At the first stop, the doors open and guests have a view down a corridor.

At the next stop, you enter another dimension, a combination of sights and sounds reminiscent of *The Twilight Zone* TV series. In fact, Disney Imagineers watched each of the 156 original *Twilight Zone* episodes at least twice for inspiration.

What happens next depends upon the whim of the Imagineers, who have programmed the drop sequence to be chillingly random. At the top (about 157 feet up), passengers can look out at the Studios below. Once the doors shut, you plummet 13 stories. The drop lasts about two seconds, but it seems a whole lot longer.

The trip takes about 5 minutes. You must be at least 40 inches tall to ride. It is not for pregnant women, those with a heart condition, or people with back and neck problems. Though thrilling, the drops are smooth. Still, if you'd rather not experience the sensation of being a human yo-yo, sit this one out.

## Rock 'n' Roller Coaster Starring Aerosmith [FP]

**BIRNBAUM'S**
**★BEST★** The fastest roller coaster in Disney World history is sure to rock your world. Rock 'n' Roller Coaster is suited for those who find Tower of Terror a tad tame.

The indoor attraction reaches a speed of nearly 60

miles per hour—in 2.8 seconds flat. Other twists include two loops and a corkscrew.

The ride's premise is this: The rock band Aerosmith has invited you to a backstage party. The only thing standing between you and the big bash is a classically chaotic Los Angeles freeway.

To get to the party on time, you'll have to zip through the nighttime L.A. streets in a stretch limo. The ride vehicles (which resemble limousines) are equipped with a high-tech sound system (five speakers per seat make for a mega-decibel ride), and the remainder of the journey features rockin' synchronized sound—adding a dramatic dimension to the coaster experience most daredevils have come to expect.

You must be free of back, neck, and heart problems to experience this topsy-turvy tour. Expectant mothers should sit this one out. Guests must be at least 48 inches tall to ride.

## Beauty and the Beast— Live on Stage

**BIRNBAUM'S**
**★BEST★** Here's the show that inspired the Broadway musical. Several times each day, Belle, Gaston, Mrs. Potts, and the rest of the cast of the Disney film *Beauty and the Beast* come to life at the 1,500-seat Theater of the Stars, near the Tower of Terror, on Sunset Boulevard.

The 30-minute show is as entertaining as they come. The staging's just right, and the music's simply addictive as it traces the classic tale—from Belle's dissatisfaction with her life in a small French town to the climactic battle between the staff of the Beast's castle and Gaston and the townspeople. Lumière and friends perform the song "Be Our Guest" with a delightful display of dancing flatware. Check a park Times Guide for performance schedule.

## The Magic of Disney Animation

This attraction gives guests an insider look at the creative process behind Disney's animated blockbusters.

The majority of the action takes place in a theater. Here, you'll be greeted by a jovial, knowledgeable host and treated to a whimsical explanation of how Disney animators bring characters to life. This segment of the tour is co-hosted by Mushu, the wisecracking little dragon from the film *Mulan*. After breezing past desks once used by animators, you'll be invited to take part in a group animation lesson. The capacity for this part of the tour is smaller than the rest, so you may have to wait a bit to get in. If you don't want to stick around, there is an exit.

Don't skip the station that lets you lend your voice to a Disney animated character or the spot that gives guests a chance to paint characters with a computer.

## Voyage of The Little Mermaid FP

One of Disney's Hollywood Studios' most popular attractions, this is a 17-minute live musical production, adapted from the Disney animated classic. The show is presented in a theater with an underwater feel. In it, many of the film's beloved animated characters, such as Flounder and Sebastian, are brought to life by puppeteers. The show opens with a lively rendition of "Under the Sea," then animated clips from the movie are shown as people join the pup-pets onstage.

Ariel is the star and performs songs from the film. Prince Eric makes an appearance, and an enormous Ursula glides across the stage to steal Ariel's voice. Of course, as in the movie, the happy ending prevails. The story line is a little bit disjointed, hopping from scene to scene, and some of the signature songs are missing. However, most viewers are familiar with the film, so this doesn't detract much from the show.

There are many special effects, including cascading water, lasers, and a lightning storm that may be a bit frightening for very young children. Note that many of the effects are best enjoyed from the middle to the rear of the theater. Keep in mind that although this is a Fastpass attraction, performances are still presented at scheduled times throughout the day.

## Playhouse Disney—Live on Stage!

Playhouse Disney fans, rejoice and put on your dancing shoes: Disney Channel favorites are on hand for a lively stage show and they invite guests to join them in the fun. Expect to see characters from *Mickey Mouse Clubhouse*, *Handy Manny*, *Little Einsteins*, and more. Among the interactive aspects of the performance is a birthday party for a very special lady—Minnie Mouse. Very young guests tend to be the most enthusiastic members of the audience.

The performance space, which resembles a working TV studio, holds large crowds (of mostly tiny people) at a time. There are just a handful of seats, but there's plenty of room to sprawl out on the carpeted floor. This show is presented at Playhouse Disney in the Animation Courtyard area of the theme park.

## Toy Story Mania! FP

**BIRNBAUM'S**
**★BEST★**

This is an energetic, interactive toy box tour with a twist: Guests wear 3-D glasses as they take aim at animated targets with toy cannons. The adventure—which opened to rave reviews in 2008—is about as high-tech as they come, yet rooted in classic midway games of skill. As points are scored, expect effusive encouragement from a colorful cast of cheerleaders—*Toy Story*'s Woody, Buzz, Hamm, Bo Peep, and of course, the Green Army Men.

Fans of Buzz Lightyear's Space Ranger Spin at the Magic Kingdom will no doubt delight in this adventure, which takes the experience of the interactive attraction to a whole new dimension. As far as skill level goes, there's something for everyone—from beginners to seasoned gamers alike. (There is a practice round to get you warmed up.) The last gaming area, Woody's Bonus Roundup, encourages guest to frantically fire their spring-action shooters in a frenetic finale. Fun for everyone!

# Studio Backlot Tour

Guests go backstage to see and experience some little-known aspects of TV and movie production on a tour of sets and prop stations. The 30-minute tour runs throughout the day.

The first stop is an outdoor effects area. This zone teaches guests how special-effects-laden water-borne scenes can be created on a set.

Guests then board trams and travel to the backlot. Trips begin with a look at the wardrobe department. More than 100 designers create costumes for Disney's movie, TV, and other projects—and, with 2.5 million garments for its workers, Disney World has the planet's largest working wardrobe. Famous costumes are on display.

The tram then passes through the camera, props, and lighting departments. A look into the scene shop reveals carpenters at work on sets that will later be finished on the soundstages.

Where in Central Florida can you find an active oil field in the middle of a barren desert canyon prone to flash floods? In Catastrophe Canyon! Expect an explosion, complete with flames so hot even riders on the far side of the tram feel them, followed by a very convincing flash flood. The road underneath the tram shifts and dips, lending more reality to the adventure.

From Catastrophe Canyon, the tram rides by the Streets of America, where reproduced building facades line urban streets. Forced perspective (the same technique that makes Cinderella Castle appear taller than it is) makes the four-story Empire State Building appear as if it were the actual 102-story structure.

# Lights, Motors, Action! Extreme Stunt Show

When it comes to action, this attraction takes the phrase "cut to the chase" quite seriously. Here, tires squeal and flames burst as cars hurtle over trucks and Jet Skis rocket from a canal. The overall guest experience is twofold. On the one hand, it is a thrilling display of seemingly death-defying feats, and on the other, it's an inside, backstage (and very loud) peek at how the movie magic happens.

Taking place in a huge theater beyond the Streets of America (on a site once occupied by Residential Street), the show is presented several times a day. Check a Times Guide for showtimes and arrive early (or get a Fastpass). Parts of the show may be too loud or intense for some small children (e.g., a stuntperson is set on fire). *This attraction operates seasonally and may not be open during your visit to the Studios.*

## American Film Institute Showcase

Though it is the final stop on the Backlot Tour, it is possible to visit this treasure chest of Hollywood memorabilia without taking the tour itself. Costumes, props, and set pieces used in recent as well as classic movies and television programs are on display in this ever-changing exhibit.

## The Great Movie Ride

Housed in a full-scale reproduction of historic Grauman's Chinese Theatre, this 19-minute attraction grabs guests' attention from the get-go. The queue area winds through a lobby and into the heart of filmmaking, where movie scenes are shown on a large screen.

The guided tour begins in an area reminiscent of the hills of Hollywood (which was once known as Hollywood-land) in its heyday. As a ride vehicle whisks guests under a vibrant marquee, they are transported to the celluloid world of yesteryear.

Guests should recognize Gene Kelly's memorable performance from *Singin' in the Rain*, in which rain seems to drench the soundstage but does not dampen the spirits of the Audio-Animatronics representation of Mr. Kelly. (Gene Kelly personally inspected his likeness.) Later, Mary Poppins and Bert the chimney sweep (Julie Andrews and Dick Van Dyke, respectively) entertain, as Mary floats from above via her magical umbrella and Bert sings from a rooftop.

From the world of musical entertainment, guests segue to adventure. James Cagney re-creates his role from *Public Enemy* as the ride proceeds along Gangster Alley. A shoot-out begins and puts guests in the midst of an ambush. An alternate route leads to a Western town, where John Wayne can be seen on horseback eyeing would-be bank robbers. As the ride vehicle glides into the spaceship from *Alien*, Officer Ripley guards the corridor while a slimy monster threatens riders from overhead. (Note that this and other scenes may upset children.)

The legendary farewell from *Casablanca* is also depicted, complete with a lifelike Rick and Ilsa. Guests are moved from the airfield to the swirling winds of Munchkinland, where a house has just fallen on the Wicked Witch of the East. Her sister, as portrayed by Margaret Hamilton, appears in a burst of smoke. This Audio-Animatronics figure is impressively realistic (and scary). As the ride draws to a close, guests view a montage of memorable moments from classic films.

## Sounds Dangerous Starring Drew Carey

As you streak around a hairpin curve, precariously positioned in the driver's seat of a speeding car, you may want to check the security of your safety belt. Don't bother. There are no seat belts. Why? As its name indicates, this attraction only *sounds* dangerous. Most of the action takes place in your head, thanks to a headset and some convincing stereo sound effects.

This 3-D audio adventure occurs inside a TV soundstage. Audience members (that's you) are on hand to watch a new show being filmed. The program, *Undercover Live*, follows a detective (played by Drew Carey) as he attempts to solve cases in the real world. Drew sports a tiny camera on his tie, so the audience can see and hear all the action.

The show, which runs continuously, lasts about 12 minutes. Given its dark and spooky moments, it may be a bit unsettling for some kids. *This attraction operates seasonally and may not be open during your visit.*

## Indiana Jones Epic Stunt Spectacular! FP

Earthquakes, fiery explosions, and assorted other dramatic events give guests some insight into the science of movie stunts and special effects at this 2,000-seat amphitheater. Stunt people re-create scenes from Indiana Jones films to demonstrate the skill required to keep audiences on the edge of their seats. But the 30-minute show isn't all flying leaps. Guests also see how the elaborate stunts are pulled off—safely—while the crew and an assistant director explain what goes on both in front of and behind the camera.

There are moments during this show when audience members might wonder if something has actually gone wrong. But by revealing tricks of the trade, the directors and stars show that what appears to be dangerous is actually a safe, controlled bit of movie-making magic.

## Star Tours FP

**BIRNBAUM'S**
**★BEST★**
This attraction, which was inspired by George Lucas's series of *Star Wars* movies, offers guests a chance to soar aboard a Star-Speeder. By synchronizing a film with the motion of the simulator, guests feel what they see.

Visitors enter an area where the famed characters R2-D2 and C-3PO are working for a galactic travel agency. They spend their time in a bustling hangar area servicing the Star Tours fleet of spacecraft. Riders board the craft for what is intended to be a leisurely trip to the Moon of Endor, but the 5-minute ride quickly develops into a harrowing flight into the depths of space. The flight is out of control from the start, as the rookie pilot proves that Murphy's Law applies to the entire universe.

This is a turbulent trip. Passengers must be free of back problems, heart conditions, motion sickness (do not ride on a full stomach), and other physical limitations. Pregnant women are not permitted to board. Guests must be at least 40 inches tall to ride.

## Muppet*Vision 3-D

**BIRNBAUM'S**
**★BEST★**
This 3-D movie is a hoot. As with so many other Disney theme park attractions, much of the appeal is in the details. A funny 12-minute pre-show gives clues about what's to come. Once inside the theater, many will notice that it looks just like the one from Jim Henson's classic TV series *The Muppet Show*. Even the two curmudgeonly

FP = FASTPASS ATTRACTION

fellows Statler and Waldorf are sitting in the balcony, bantering with each other and offering their typically critical commentary on the show.

The production comes directly from Muppet Labs, presided over by Dr. Bunsen Honeydew—and his long-suffering assistant, Beaker—and introduces a new character, Waldo, the "Spirit of 3-D." Among the high-lights is Miss Piggy's solo, which Bean Bunny turns into quite a fiasco. Sam Eagle's grand finale leads to trouble as a veritable war breaks out, culminating with a cannon blast to the screen from the rear balcony, courtesy of everyone's favorite Swedish Chef.

The 3-D effects, enjoyable as they may be, are only part of the show: There are appearances by Muppet characters, fireworks, and lots of details built into the walls of the huge theater. Including the pre-show, expect to spend about 30 minutes with Kermit and company. Shows run continuously throughout the day.

## Honey, I Shrunk the Kids Movie Set Adventure

The set for the backyard scenes of the classic Disney movie has been re-created as an oversize, soft-surface playground. Enter it and experience the world from an ant's perspective.

Blades of grass soar 30 feet high, paper clips are as tall as trees, and toys are practically big enough to live in. There are caves to explore (under the giant mushrooms) and climbing opportunities (tremendous tree stumps and sprawling spiderwebs are among the better ones). The props make everyone look and feel as though they were, indeed, shrunk by *Honey, I Shrunk the Kids'* Professor Wayne Szalinski. It holds the most appeal for youngsters.

## The American Idol Experience

**BIRNBAUM'S**
**★BEST★** Inspired by TV's *American Idol*, this interactive show invites park guests to sing their hearts out in a realistic re-creation of the show. Simon and Paula aren't here, but Disney's judges are quite discerning. What's at stake (besides honor)? A chance to audition for the real *American Idol*—without having to wait in line. No kidding!

# Entertainment

In these parts, it's always showtime! While specifics may change, the following list is a good indication of the Studios' stage presence.

**BLOCK PARTY BASH:** A high-energy extravaganza, this processional is led by *Toy Story*'s Green Army men and features characters from Disney•Pixar films, plus acrobats, rolling stages, trampolines, and audience participation.

**HIGH SCHOOL MUSICAL SHOW:** Feeling fabulous? Make a beeline for the oversize Sorcerer's Hat on Hollywood Boulevard for this interactive *High School Musical*–inspired song and dance party. It's presented several times daily.

**STREETMOSPHERE CHARACTERS:** This troupe of performers infuses Hollywood Boulevard with old-time Tinseltown ambience. Would-be starlets searching for their big break, fans seeking guests' autographs, and gossip columnists chasing leads entertain daily.

## Fantasmic!

**BIRNBAUM'S BEST** Fantasmic!, a 26-minute musical production, plays several times a week (more during peak times of year) at The Hollywood Hills Amphitheater on Sunset Boulevard. A dramatic mix of fireworks, fountains, lasers, and Disney characters, it

offers a peek into the dream world of Mickey Mouse.

Seating begins about 90 minutes before show-time—though some guests line up even earlier. Check a Times Guide for the schedule. We recommend sitting toward the back—the view is good and it's easier to get out after the show. There is standing room, too.

After the finale, plan to sit for a bit. It can take 20 minutes for the crowd to exit the theater. Note that parts of this show have been known to frighten small children. (Those Disney villains can be scary!)

**Timing Tip:** On nights when Fantasmic! is presented twice, see the late show—it's often easier to get into.

# Hot Tips

- Some attractions keep shorter hours than the park itself. Check a Times Guide when you arrive. It lists current hours and schedules.

- Check the Studios' Tip Board often to get an idea of showtimes and crowds.

- Snag a spot along Hollywood Boulevard about 20 to 30 minutes before the Block Party Bash parade.

- See Rock 'n' Roller Coaster, Tower of Terror, Voyage of The Little Mermaid, and Toy Story Mania early in the day, before crowds build up.

- Think you've mastered Toy Story Mania? Think again. Many of the targets, when struck, reveal a new and more valuable target. There is at least one such target in each game area.

- Tower of Terror is a popular attraction with long lines. Use Fastpass whenever possible. And never ride immediately after a meal.

- The line for The Great Movie Ride is generally the longest early in the morning and immediately following the afternoon parade.

- The shops on Hollywood Boulevard are open a half hour past park closing.

- Park-hoppers, take note: There is a water taxi link between Disney's Hollywood Studios and Epcot. The boat docks to the left as you exit the Studios. You may also reach Epcot, as well as all other parks, by bus. Athletes may choose to walk. (It'll take about 20 to 30 minutes to make the trip on foot.)

- Many attractions and shows stop admitting guests prior to the park's closing time (and some don't open until a few hours after the park does).

Check a Times Guide for schedules. Attractions that you may enter up until the very last minute include Rock 'n' Roller Coaster, The Twilight Zone Tower of Terror, The Great Movie Ride, Muppet*Vision 3-D, Toy Story Mania, and Star Tours.

- On nights when Fantasmic is presented twice, plan to see the late show (it's usually easier to get a seat). Afterward, as the masses exit the park, spend some time browsing the shops on Hollywood Boulevard that keep their doors—and their cash registers—open after hours.

- If you choose to skip Fantasmic, plan to exit the park before the show ends. This way, you'll avoid the inevitable bottleneck at the exit. If you're watching the show, consider making your exit before the big finale.

- If you plan to ride Rock 'n' Roller Coaster, be sure to stash your stuff in a locker first. There's no place to store loose articles in the ride vehicles. Lockers are located near the entrance to the park.

- As you board the tram for the Studio Backlot Tour, know that guests on the left side tend to get spritzed (though not soaked) with water in Catastrophe Canyon. Just a warning.

- Parts of the Great Movie Ride are scary for young children. The scenes from *Alien* and *The Wizard of Oz* are especially unsettling for tykes.

- To ensure that the Disney magic is uninterrupted for you and those around you, turn off your wireless phone (or at the very least, put it on vibrate). You're on vacation—don't let the real world ruin the fun.

- The Osborne Family Spectacle of Lights—a wildly popular display of millions of lights "performing" in synchronized motion with music—is presented in the Streets of America area of the park during the Christmas holiday season. (It starts in November and usually runs through early January.) For updates on this beloved holiday event, call 407-824-4321.

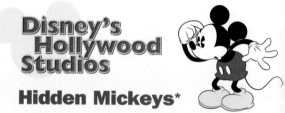

# Disney's Hollywood Studios

## Hidden Mickeys*

These are some of the most popular "Hidden Mickeys" at Disney's Hollywood Studios. How many can you find? Check the box when you spot each one.

♥ **Front Entrance Gates:** This is an easy one. Simply look for Mr. Mouse in the grillwork of the gates near the turnstiles. An even easier one? Look up to spot the water tower that's become a symbol of the park. It's capped with a gigantic pair of Mouse Ears! (Hence the name Earfful Tower.) ❑

♥ **Rock 'n' Roller Coaster:** In the pre-show room, look on the floor on the right side of the room just in front of the guitar stand to see some wire coiled into a Hidden Mickey. ❑

♥ **Star Tours:** As you enter the interior queue, pay close attention for three Hidden Mickeys. One is on the immediate right wall—you'll find it on a poster that says Phone Directory. The other two are on the left wall, on an Employment Opportunities notice on the lower-right side of the bulletin board. ❑

♥ **Sounds Dangerous Starring Drew Carey:** Look to the left of the Sounds Dangerous attraction to find the Radio Disney sign. The "O" has a Hidden Mickey in the center. ❑

♥ **Twilight Zone™ Tower of Terror:** As you watch the pre-show video presentation, pay close attention to the "disappearing guests." The little girl is clutching a plush Mickey Mouse. ❑

♥ **Mama Melrose's Ristorante Italiano:** As you enter, look for the Dalmatian in the waiting area. One of its spots is Mickey-shaped. ❑

❤ **Stage 1 Company Store:** Inside the store, locate a tall bureau with paint cans on the top (the shelves are covered with Disney hats for sale). On the desk area, you'll find a green Hidden Mickey. ❏

❤ **The Hollywood Brown Derby:** Look for two hidden Mickeys in the cloud mural outside the restaurant. One is on the left side, above the red Stage 5 sign, and the other is on the far upper right-hand side. ❏

❤ **Cover Story:** There is a sign in the window of this Hollywood Boulevard shop that says "Melrose." Find it, then look below it for a pattern that creates many Hidden Mickeys in the store's structure. ❏

❤ **The Great Movie Ride:** Pay attention to the posters on the left as you enter the gangster area of the ride. When you see a poster for the film *The Public Enemy*, look in the lower left corner to find Mickey's shoes (they are brown) and his tail poking out. You can also spot Mickey in the Indiana Jones room (aka The Well of Souls). He's in the hieroglyphics on the wall to the left of the ride vehicle. ❏

❤ **Studio Backlot Tour:** After the stunt demonstration, as you enter the prop shop, pay attention to a yellow refrigerator on the right side in the first aisle to find a silver Hidden Mickey. During the tour, check out Walt Disney's plane. One Mickey is rather obvious, the other is a bit more subtle. ❏

❤ **Muppet*Vision 3-D:** As you exit, you'll see a poster detailing "5 Reasons to Return" your 3-D glasses. Take a close look at the artwork beside number 2. It has a Hidden Mickey! Outside of the attraction, "Director" Gonzo is balancing on a Hidden Mickey statue in the fountain. ❏

❤ **Pizza Planet:** First, find the mural inside this arcade/fast-food restaurant near Muppet*Vision 3-D. (It's in the arcade area.) Then locate the moon in the mural. Can you spot Mickey's profile? (Hint: He's just to the left of the alien hanging from the ceiling.) ❏

*\* Specifics may change during 2010.*

# Studios Dining

Should you find yourself without reservations to a table-service eatery, grab a bite at one of many quick-service establishments. The list* of nosh-worthy spots includes the following:

**ABC COMMISSARY:** Located near the Great Movie Ride, this spacious restaurant features international cuisine. Expect items such as Cuban sandwiches, Asian salad, fish and chips, and burgers.

**BACKLOT EXPRESS:** This "old craft shop" Star Tours' neighbor serves burgers, hot dogs, salads, turkey sandwiches, and vegetable paninis. For dessert, there's strawberry parfait.

**PIZZA PLANET:** Kid-friendly pizzas—plain, pepperoni, or veggie—are the main attraction here. Salads are also an option. You'll find it inside the Pizza Planet Arcade, across from the Muppets.

**STARRING ROLLS CAFE:** Specialty sandwiches, croissants, bagels, and pastries are the specialties of this house. They brew a decent cup of coffee, too.

**STUDIO CATERING CO.:** Situated next to the Honey, I Shrunk the Kids Movie Set Adventure, this eatery serves up barbecued pulled pork subs, chicken Caesar wraps, chili dogs, and grilled chicken.

**SUNSET RANCH MARKET:** The cluster of stands on Sunset Boulevard offers selections such as pepperoni pizza, hot Italian deli sandwiches, salads, cheese burgers, chicken strips, veggie burgers, and soup. Other options include turkey legs, pulled pork subs, taco salads, and fresh fruit. (We're suckers for the Granny Smith slices with caramel dipping sauce.)

* Note that while all of the above participate in the Disney Dining Plan, ABC Commissary and Starring Rolls Cafe are the only places listed here that offer breakfast items.

# Disney's Animal Kingdom

With a mix of lush landscapes, thrilling attractions, and close encounters with exotic animals, this is clearly a theme park raised to a different level of excitement. Here, guests do more than just watch the action—they live it. They become paleontologists, explorers, and students of nature. And if, by doing so, they leave with nothing more than a great big smile, Disney will have accomplished one of its major goals. But many guests come away with a little bit more: a renewed sense of respect for our planet and for the life forms we share it with (not to mention a few boffo souvenirs).

The attractions at Disney's Animal Kingdom are meant to engage, entertain, and inspire. They immerse guests in a tropical landscape and introduce them to creatures from the past and present—as well as a few that exist only in our collective imagination.

The park, which is accredited by the American Zoo and Aquarium Association, is home to more than 1,700 animals representing 250 different species. Most of the creatures are of the animate variety, as opposed to the Audio-Animatronics kind. Despite that, you won't see many beasts behind bars here. Instead, you'll go on safari and see a menagerie of wild critters living in spacious habitats, with remarkably few separations visible to the naked eye.

The following pages will help you get the most out of your visit to Disney's Animal Kingdom. It is, after all, a jungle out there.

# Getting Oriented

Though Disney's Animal Kingdom encompasses about five times the area of its Magic counterpart, one need not be in training for the Olympics to tackle it. (Most of the land is reserved for non-homo-sapien critters.) By all estimates, pedestrians rack up about the same mileage in one day here as they do in a day at Epcot.

The park's layout is relatively simple: a series of sections, or "lands," connected to a central hub. In this case, the hub is Discovery Island, an island surrounded by a river, and home to the Tree of Life, the park's icon. A set of bridges connects Discovery Island with other lands: the Oasis, DinoLand U.S.A., Asia, Africa, and Camp Minnie-Mickey.

As you pass through Animal Kingdom's entrance plaza, you approach the Oasis. Feel free to meander at a leisurely pace, absorbing the soothing ambience of a thick, elaborate jungle, or you can proceed more quickly and plan to revisit this relaxing region later on. Each of several pathways deposits you at the foot of a bridge leading to Discovery Island. As you emerge from the Oasis, you'll see the Tree of Life, a 14-story Disney-made tree, looming ahead. The tree, which stands near the middle of the island, is surrounded by Discovery Island Trails. Off to the southwest is the character-laden land known as Camp Minnie-Mickey.

To the southeast lies DinoLand U.S.A., home of prehistoric animals, a fossil dig, a high-spirited stage show called Finding Nemo—The Musical, and an attraction that's sure to induce a mammoth adrenaline surge: Dinosaur. Behind Discovery Island and to the northwest is Africa, where guests may go on an African safari, explore a nature trail, and take the Wildlife Express train to Rafiki's Planet Watch, the park's research and education center.

Asia is northeast of Discovery Island. Here, guests come face-to-face with the Yeti, aka Abominable Snowman, on the Expedition Everest thrill ride; encounter real tigers on the exotic Maharajah Jungle Trek; and take a daring journey through the rainforest on a raft at the splashy Kali River Rapids.

## HOW TO GET THERE

**By car:** Take Exit 65 off I-4. Then follow the signs to Disney's Animal Kingdom. Trams run between the parking lot and the main entrance.

**By WDW Transportation:** From all Walt Disney World resorts: buses. From Downtown Disney: bus to any resort or the TTC, then transfer to an Animal Kingdom bus. From the Magic Kingdom: ferry or monorail to the TTC, then bus to Animal Kingdom. From Epcot, Disney's Hollywood Studios, and the resorts on Hotel Plaza Boulevard: buses.

## PARKING

All-day parking at Animal Kingdom is $12 for day visitors (free to Walt Disney World resort guests with presentation of resort ID). Trams circulate regularly, providing transportation from the parking area to the park entrance. Be sure to note the section and aisle in which you park. Also, be aware that the parking ticket allows for re-entry to the parking area throughout the day.

## HOURS

Although hours are subject to change, the gates are generally open daily from about 9 A.M. until about an hour after dusk. During some holiday periods and the summer months, hours may change. It's best to arrive up to a half hour before the official opening time.

# Park Primer

## BABY FACILITIES

Changing tables and facilities for nursing mothers can be found at the Baby Care Center on Discovery Island, near Creature Comforts. It's also possible to purchase certain necessities, such as formula and diapers, at this facility.

## CAMERA NEEDS

Camera supplies and disposable cameras can be purchased at Garden Gate Gifts, Disney Outfitters, Duka La Filimu, Mombasa Marketplace, and Chester and Hester's Dinosaur Treasures. Images may be transferred to CDs at Garden Gate Gifts. Note that film processing is not available.

## DISABILITY INFORMATION

Nearly all attractions, shops, and restaurants are accessible to guests using wheelchairs. Additional services are available for guests with visual or hearing disabilities. The *Guide for Guests with Disabilities* provides a detailed overview of the services available. Pick one up at Guest Relations near the entrance.

## FIRST AID

Minor medical problems can be handled at the First Aid Center, located on Discovery Island on the northwest side of the Tree of Life, near Creature Comforts.

## INFORMATION

Guest Relations, located just inside the park entrance, is equipped with guidemaps, Times Guides, and a helpful staff. Guidemaps are also available in many shops.

## LOCKERS

Lockers are found just inside the main entrance area, near Guest Relations. They are available for a fee. (Hold on to your receipt if you plan to park-hop.)

## LOST & FOUND

The department is located at Guest Relations, just inside the park entrance. To report lost items after your visit, call 407-824-4245.

## LOST CHILDREN

Report lost children at the park's Baby Care Center, near Creature Comforts on Discovery Island, or alert the closest Disney employee to the matter.

## MONEY MATTERS

There is an ATM (automated teller machine) at the entrance to the park. Currency exchange can be handled at Guest Relations. Disney Dollars are also available at Guest Relations (Disney Dollars are accepted as cash throughout most of Walt Disney World). In addition to cash, credit cards (American Express, Diner's Club, Discover Card, JCB, Visa, MasterCard, and Disney Visa Card), Disney gift cards, traveler's checks, and Disney resort IDs are accepted for admission and merchandise, and for meals at most restaurants. Some snack carts accept cash only.

## PACKAGE PICKUP

Shops can arrange for purchases to be sent to Garden Gate Gifts for later pickup (packages should be ready for pickup about three hours after purchase). The service is free.

## SAME-DAY RE-ENTRY

Be sure to retain your ticket if you plan to return later the same day. It is no longer necessary to have your hand stamped.

## SECURITY CHECK

Guests entering Disney theme parks are subject to a security check. Expect backpacks, parcels, purses, etc. to be searched.

## STROLLERS & WHEELCHAIRS

Strollers, wheelchairs, and Electric Convenience Vehicles (ECVs) may be rented at Garden Gate Gifts. "Length-of-Stay" rentals yield a daily discount. Quantities are limited (and they run out early in the day). Keep your receipt; it may be used the same day to get a replacement here or at the other theme parks.

## TIP BOARD

There is a Tip Board on Discovery Island. Check it to learn current wait times for popular park attractions.

# The Oasis

Though not a full-fledged "land" per se, this small jungle simply oozes atmosphere. (When searching for the naturally camouflaged creatures, remember to look up occasionally.) As park visitors walk along the pathways, they may catch glimpses of different kinds of animals, from deer and iguanas to anteaters and birds. As in the rest of the Animal Kingdom, there is the illusion that guests are walking among wildlife.

Once you've passed through the Oasis, you will come to a bridge. It leads to Discovery Island, an area at the center of Animal Kingdom and the hub from which all other realms of the park may be reached.

Discovery Island is defined by the brilliant colors, tropical surroundings, and equatorial architecture of Africa and the South Pacific. The facades of the buildings are all carved and painted based on the art of nations from around the world. Don't fail to notice all the bright, whimsical folk-art images representing various members of the animal kingdom.

By far the most striking element on Discovery Island is the Tree of Life. It is on the map, but chances are you'll have no trouble finding it—as tall as a 14-story building, the Tree of Life is hard to miss.

## Discovery Island
### The Tree of Life

The Tree of Life is the dramatic 145-foot icon of Disney's Animal Kingdom. The imposing tree, with its swaying limbs and gnarled trunk, looks an awful lot like the real thing—from a distance. Up close, it's clear that this is a most unusual bit of greenery. Covered with more than 325 animal images, it is a swirling tapestry of carved figures, painstakingly assembled

by a team of artisans. The tree, though inorganic, stands as a symbol of the connected nature of life on Earth. We think Joyce Kilmer would have approved.

**DISCOVERY ISLAND TRAILS:** Walkways that snake around the Tree of Life allow guests to get a close-up view of the trunk and even play a game of "spot the animals." (The spiraling animal images go all the way to the top of the tree. You'll need binoculars if you hope to see them all.) Scattered about the tree's base is a variety of animal habitats. The trails are accessible from several points around the tree.

**IT'S TOUGH TO BE A BUG!:** **FP** Inside the trunk of the Tree of Life is a 430-seat auditorium featuring an eight-minute, animated 3-D movie augmented by some surprising "4-D" effects. The stars of the show are the world's most abundant inhabitants—insects. They creep, crawl, and demonstrate why, someday, they just might inherit the Earth. It's a bug's-eye view of the trials and tribulations of their multi-legged world.

As guests enter "The Tree of Life Repertory Theater," the orchestra can be heard warming up amid the sounds of chirping crickets. When Flik, the emcee (and star of *A Bug's Life*), makes his first appearance, he dubs audience members honorary bugs and instructs them to don their bug eyes (3-D glasses). What follows is a manic, often humorous, revue.

**Note:** The combination of intense special effects and frequent darkness tends to frighten toddlers and young children. In addition, anyone leery of spiders, roaches, and their ilk is advised to skip the performance, or risk being seriously bugged.

# Africa

This 110-acre, truer-than-life replica of an African savanna is packed with pachyderms, giraffes, hippos, and other wild beasts. All guests enter Africa through Harambe, a village based on a modern East African coastal town. It is the dining and shopping center of Animal Kingdom's Africa.

The instant you walk across the bridge to Harambe, you are transported to Africa. Everything here is authentic, from architecture to landscaping to the merchandise in the marketplace. The result was achieved after Disney Imagineers made countless trips to the continent. After seven years of observing the real thing, they re-created it here in North America.

## Kilimanjaro Safaris FP

The Kilimanjaro Safaris has something for everyone: beautiful landscapes, majestic, free-roaming animals, and a thrilling adventure. It is everything you may expect from a trip to Africa, and a whole lot more.

The 18-minute safari begins with a brief introduction from a guide who does double duty as your driver. Once you climb aboard the ride vehicle, look at the plates above the seat in front of you. They will help you identify the animals you see.

As the vehicle travels along dirt roads, you'll spot free-roaming wild animals: zebras, gazelles, hippos, elephants, warthogs, rhinos, lions, and more. Some animals wander near the vehicle, and others cross its path. (Only harmless critters can approach.

Others, such as lions and cheetahs, only *appear* to invade your safe, personal space.)

The majesty of the Serengeti may lull you into a state of serenity, but it's merely the calm before the storm. You'll soon be jostled and jolted as the vehicle crosses pothole-filled terrain and rickety bridges—one of which puts you close to sunbathing crocodiles.

The safari experience takes a dramatic turn when a band of renegade ivory poachers is discovered hunting for elephants. Your guide chases the outlaws and takes you along for the ride. If you're prone to motion sickness, back trouble, or have other physical limitations, you may want to sit this one out. The ride is a bumpy one.

## Pangani Forest Exploration Trail

This self-guided trail winds past communities of gorillas and other rare African animals. Access it at the end of the Kilimanjaro Safaris or by the entrance in Harambe.

The first major stop on the trail—the name of which translates to "place of enchantment" in Swahili—is the Research Station. The station contains exhibits, including naked mole rats. Just outside are a free-flight aviary and an aquarium teeming with fish. Not far away is the hippo exhibit, which provides close-up views of hippopotamuses both in and out of water.

Farther along the trail, there is a scenic overlook point, where you can get an unobstructed view of the African savanna. This is also known as the "Timon" exhibit, featuring a family of perky meerkats. Afterward, you may catch an up-close glimpse (through a glass wall) of a gorilla or two.

As you come to the end of the suspension bridge, you'll find yourself in a beautiful green valley. Congratulations! You've finally reached the gorilla area—an experience well worth the wait. (Note that you may have to wait a little bit longer for that first gorilla sighting. Our evolutionary cousins have been known to play hide-and-seek in the lush vegetation.)

## Rafiki's Planet Watch

On the east side of the village of Harambe is the Harambe Train Station. That's where you board the Wildlife Express and experience a behind-the-scenes look at the park while en route to Rafiki's Planet Watch.

As part of the 5½-minute trip, you'll glide past the buildings where elephants, rhinos, and giraffes sleep at night. A guide narrates throughout the trip. All guests disembark at the Rafiki's Planet Watch station. (You must reboard the train to return to Harambe.) It's about a 5-minute walk to the exhibits.

This area is the park's conservation headquarters. Exhibits are geared to spark curiosity about wildlife and conservation efforts around the world. The highlights:

**Habitat Habit!:** An outdoor discovery trail that yields glimpses of cotton-top tamarins and helpful hints on how to share our world with all members of the animal kingdom.

**Affection Section:** An animal encounter area with critters to see and touch. Most of the animals are exotic breeds of familiar petting-zoo types: goats, sheep, pigs, etc. However, this is still an enjoyable experience for young guests.

**Conservation Station:** The center of Disney's effort to promote wildlife conservation awareness. Inside, you'll find:

*Animal Cams:* Guest-operated video cameras that observe animals throughout Animal Kingdom as they go about their daily business.

*Animal Health & Care:* A peek at veterinary labs and research facilities.

*Eco Heroes:* A set of touch-sensitive video kiosks that allow guests to interact with famous biologists and conservationists.

*EcoWeb:* A computer link to conservation organizations around the world.

*Rafiki's Planet Watch Video:* An interactive video, hosted by Rafiki, that gives guests information about endangered animals.

*Song of the Rainforest:* A thoroughly entertaining "3-D" audio show that surrounds guests with sounds of the rainforest.

## Asia

On the far side of a Himalayan-style bridge lies the village of Anandapur (Sanskrit for "place of delight"). The buildings' design was inspired by structures in Thailand, Indonesia, and other Asian countries known for their rich architectural history.

**BIRNBAUM'S**
# ★BEST★ Kali River Rapids FP

Before guests board rafts at Kali (pronounced *KAH-lee*) River Rapids, a wise voice admonishes that "the river is like life itself, full of mysterious twists and turns." What the voice *doesn't* say is that this particular river is also full of splashing water and a blazing inferno.

Guests begin the journey in the offices of Kali River Rapids Expeditions, a river rafting company. A slide show offers details on the sometimes unscrupulous business of logging—how it has ravaged the rainforest and deprived animals of their habitats. However, thanks to ecotourism (among other things), there is hope.

A 12-seater raft whisks "ecotourists" up a watery ramp and through an arching tunnel of bamboo. It proceeds onward, through a hazy mist and past remnants of an ancient shrine. As the raft moves along curves of the river, guests enjoy views of undisturbed rainforest.

The tranquility is shattered by a startling sight. A chunk of forest has been gutted by humans. On both sides of the river, the forest has vanished. As guests absorb the image, they are besieged by more disturbing sights and sounds. Straight ahead, the river is choked with a tangled arch of burning logs—and the raft is headed straight for it. Suddenly, the rainforest isn't the only thing endangered.

Kali River Rapids is a drenching experience. Should you wish to repel as much precipitation as possible, pack a plastic poncho.

**Note:** This is a bumpy adventure. It is not for pregnant women, those with a heart condition, people with back or neck problems, or anyone who wishes to stay dry. Minimum height requirement: 38 inches. Everyone on the raft receives a thorough drenching. Stash valuables with a non-riding member of your party.

*DISNEY'S ANIMAL KINGDOM*

# BIRNBAUM'S ★BEST★ Maharajah Jungle Trek

Welcome to the jungle! The Maharajah Jungle Trek is a self-guided walking tour of a tropical paradise, complete with roaming tigers, gushing waterfalls, and dense greenery. Throughout the expedition, trekkers encounter a deluge of flora and fauna typically found in the rainforests of Southeast Asia. Tapirs, Komodo dragons, and a conglomeration of colorful birds call this corner of Animal Kingdom home. Majestic Asian tigers can be spotted stalking ancient ruins, strategically separated from would-be prey. Deer and antelope graze and frolic nearby, blissfully oblivious of their fearsome neighbors' proximity.

About midway through the thicket stands a rustic, tin-roofed assembly hall. Step inside to witness giant fruit bats showing off their six-foot wingspans. As you look through the windows, thinking that the crystal-clear glass was cleaned by a super-diligent window washer, think again. There is no glass in some of the windows—and, therefore, *nothing* separating you from the giant creatures fluttering about on the other side. What keeps the big bats from getting up close and personal with guests? They're a lot less interested in humans than we are in them. (Can't say that we blame them.) Some viewing areas are adorned with wire or glass—for guests who are more comfortable with a bat buffer.

## Flights of Wonder

A 1,000-seat, open-air theater, the Caravan Stage features performances by actors wearing nothing but feathers and the occasional crown. Members of more than 20 different bird species have starring roles in Flights of Wonder, a high-flying celebration of the winged wonders of the world. Hawks, owls, falcons, and even chickens have been known to awe spectators as they swoop, soar, and strut their stuff in each 20-minute performance. Some demonstrate how they hunt. Others display their grape-grabbing or money-grubbing talents. Check a Times Guide for the daily schedule. This show has morphed quite a bit from its original incarnation. It's a hoot!

## BIRNBAUM'S BEST ★ Expedition Everest

Walt Disney World's mountain range is a bit more intense these days, as the world's tallest mountain—Everest—has risen from the peaceful village of Serka Zong in Animal Kingdom's Asia. Like its sister peaks, Space, Splash, and Big Thunder, this E-ticket precipice promises to deliver "coaster thrills, spills, and chills." Does it deliver on that promise? Boy, does it ever.

The attraction features an old tea train chugging and churning as it climbs up and around snowcapped peaks. Suddenly, the track comes to an end in a

gnarled mess of twisted metal. Lurching forward and backward, the train hurtles through caverns and icy canyons before depositing guests in the presence of the legendary Yeti (aka the Abominable Snowman)—who's not too happy that you've scaled the mountain he so fiercely protects.

Feeling up to the challenge of a dramatic, high-speed train ride? If you are free of heart, back, and neck problems, are not pregnant, have no fear of heights (or Abominable snowpeople), go for it. As always, never eat right before experiencing a ride as topsy-turvy as this one. Minimum height requirement: 44 inches.

## DinoLand U.S.A.

If the look and feel of DinoLand U.S.A. seems familiar, there's a reason: It was designed to capture the flavor of roadside America. It is a mixture of culture and kitsch—the likes of which you might stumble upon during a cross-country road trip. Here, you'll come face to face with fossil fanatics, jump into gigantic footprints, and browse through a roadside souvenir stand, where you can pick up some dinosaur mementos for the folks back home.

The dinosaurs that dwell here, though often quite animated, are all of the inanimate variety. But do keep your eyes peeled for a few prehistoric life-forms that actually *live* in this land. That is, for real creatures that exist in the here and now, but whose ancestors kept company with the likes of the carnotaurus and its cousins from the Cretaceous era.

## The Boneyard

The Boneyard gives very young guests an opportunity to dig for fossils in a discovery-oriented playground. They will excavate the ancient bones of a mammoth in this re-creation of a paleontological dig (think huge sandbox). They will also unearth clues that may help them solve the mystery of how and when the creature met its untimely demise.

There are other bone-related activities here, too. Kids can bang out a primitive tune on a bony xylophone (it's located near the car; to make a sound, simply press on a rib), zip down prehistoric slides, and work their way through a fossil-filled maze. While exploring, watch your step: If you accidentally wander into a giant dinosaur footprint, you'll be greeted with an ominous roar.

## Chester & Hester's Dino-Rama!

A colorful land-within-a-land, Chester and Hester's is an area best suited for young thrill seekers. Located just beyond The Boneyard playground, this carnival-like zone features midway games and two rides—Primeval Whirl and TriceraTop Spin.

**PRIMEVAL WHIRL:** 🄵🄿 A small roller coaster (with spinning cars) that seems to have been plucked from a

traveling fair, this ride has a familiar feel to it. By all means, give it a whirl—it's a truly wild ride. You must be at least 48 inches tall to spin. Skip it if you are pregnant or susceptible to motion sickness.

**TRICERATOP SPIN:** The ride is apt to please fans of the Magic Kingdom's Dumbo the Flying Elephant, and the Magic Carpets of Aladdin. Guests ride in one of the 16 flying dinos, each of which resembles an over-size tin toy. It's tame when compared to its Dinosaur attraction neighbor, but worth checking out—especially for little dinosaur groupies.

**BIRNBAUM'S ★BEST★ Dinosaur** FP This dizzying adventure begins with guests being strapped into vehicles and catapulted back in time to complete a dangerous, albeit noble, mission: to rescue the last iguanodon—a 16-foot plant-eating dinosaur—and bring him back to the present. The iguanodon, which lived more than 65 million years ago (during the Cretaceous period), just might hold the answer to the mysterious disappearance of his dino brethren.

**FP** = FASTPASS ATTRACTION

99

Throughout the frenetic quest to locate the elusive iguanodon, you cling to an out-of-control vehicle while dodging blazing meteors and a mix of friendly and ferocious dinosaurs. Soon you encounter the carnotaurus —a fearsome, carnivorous dinosaur.

This 3½-minute attraction offers more than a thrill a minute. You rocket through time, are practically pelted by meteors, and narrowly escape becoming a dino dinner as the carnotaurus suddenly turns the tables and chases after *you*.

This is an extremely rough (and dark) attraction. You must be at least 40 inches tall to experience it. It is not for pregnant women, those with a heart condition, or people with back or neck problems. Small kids will certainly be frightened.

## Finding Nemo—The Musical

DinoLand is just about as far off Broadway as one could be. Yet this show's got the ingredients of a Broadway favorite (albeit an abbreviated one): beloved characters (i.e., Marlin, the overprotective clownfish dad; Nemo, his curious son; and Dory, the endearing royal blue tang with short-term memory loss); original songs by a Tony-winning composer (Robert Lopez); dancers; acrobats; and the theatrical puppetry of Michael Curry (who designed the richly detailed character puppets seen in the Broadway version of Disney's *The Lion King*). You can catch this 30-minute show at the enclosed and air-conditioned Theater in the Wild. Check a Times Guide for showtimes—and get there early. It appeals to all ages.

## Camp Minnie-Mickey

What would a theme park be without a gregarious cast of handshaking characters? You will find the patented Disney character experience in all of its animated glory in Camp Minnie-Mickey. Set in a dense forest, this land is a summer camp frequented by Mickey Mouse and his pals. It is also the home of a rousing stage show starring the cast of *The Lion King*. Check a Times Guide for schedules.

# BIRNBAUM'S BEST Festival of the Lion King

In addition to rustling up grubs in Camp Minnie-Mickey, the talented cast of *The Lion King* performs a 30-minute stage show in the Lion King Theater.

Presented in the round, this lavish revue is as bright and boisterous as they come. The dramatic opening features a parade of performers in colorful animal costumes. What follows is an intriguing, energetic interpretation of the film,

including songs, dances, and acrobatics. With the exception of Timon, who plays himself, lead characters are portrayed by humans draped in bold African costumes.

**Timing Tip:** Although this enclosed theater accommodates nearly 1,400 guests at a time, we recommend arriving at least 30 minutes before the performance time. Take our word for it: It's worth the wait.

## Greeting Trails

Tucked within Camp Minnie-Mickey (across from Festival of the Lion King) are several short trails. At the end of each one, you'll find very special furry friends: Disney characters. Mickey, Minnie, Donald, Goofy, and many of their pals are on hand to greet Animal Kingdom guests at special open-air huts. Different characters appear throughout the day. Don't forget to bring cameras and autograph books.

**AFRICAN ENTERTAINMENT:** Contemporary sounds of Africa often fill the air as bands serenade guests passing through the village of Harambe. Storytellers have been known to perform animal tales from time to time.

**ANIMAL ENCOUNTERS:** Enjoy up-close encounters with some tiny members of the animal kingdom as they wander the park with their human keepers.

**MICKEY'S JAMMIN' JUNGLE PARADE:** Animal Kingdom celebrates the wonders of the natural world in this peppy parade. It features favorite Disney characters—including Mickey Mouse, Minnie Mouse, Goofy, Donald Duck, and Rafiki—cruising in jazzy jalopies. Stilt-walkers and puppets put in appearances, too. Check a Times Guide for the parade schedule.

# Hot Tips

- Arrive at the park about 20 minutes before park opening time. Animal Kingdom often kicks off the day with "The Adventure Begins"—a character-laden musical celebration. It's a very Disney way to start the day.

- Island Mercantile on Discovery Island stays open a half hour after the park closes.

- Most of Animal Kingdom's attractions take place outdoors. Don't become overheated! Make a point of slipping into an air-conditioned shop or restaurant from time to time to cool off.

- Narrow, winding paths, grooved pavement, and hilly terrain make this the most challenging Disney theme park in which to navigate a wheelchair.

- Check the Animal Kingdom Tip Board often to get an idea of showtimes and crowds.

- The line for Kilimanjaro Safaris tends to dwindle a bit by midday—see it then. (The experience is enjoyable at any time of day, and contrary to popular belief, the animals' energy level does not peak in the A.M.)

- Get a Fastpass for Expedition Everest first thing in the morning—they are often gone before lunchtime.

- Rainforest Cafe stays open later than the park does.

- When the weather gets steamy, keep a refillable water bottle with you at all times.

- If you plan to park-hop, Animal Kingdom is a good park at which to begin the day.

- After the Magic Kingdom, this park has the most tot-pleasing shows and attractions.

# Disney's Animal Kingdom

## Hidden Mickeys*

These are some of the most popular "Hidden Mickeys" at Animal Kingdom. How many can you find? Check the box when you spot each one!

♥ **Expedition Everest:** To find this Hidden Mickey, grab a Fastpass for Expedition Everest and then pay attention to the Yeti Museum room in the queue. In the second display of expedition artifacts and supplies, look for a lantern on a shelf—three dents in the metal form a sideways Hidden Mickey. ❏

♥ **Kilimanjaro Safaris:** Pay close attention to the flamingo pond on your left just after you enter elephant country. The center island is shaped like a Hidden Mickey (sit toward the left of the ride vehicle for the best view). ❏

♥ **Maharajah Jungle Trek:** There are more than ten Hidden Mickeys throughout this jungle trek, but we suggest hunting for these two to start. Inside the first archway near the tiger exhibit, pay attention to the mural on the left and look for three leaves that form a Hidden Mickey underneath the extended arm of a king. Now walk to the second arch and look at the mural on the right to find a Hidden Mickey in the clouds. ❏

♥ **Pangani Forest Exploration Trail:** While not a Hidden *Mickey*, the Hidden Jafar found in this trail is well worth searching for. Just past the gorilla viewing area, you'll reach a suspension bridge. Look directly to your right and you'll see a huge 3-D head of Jafar carved out of the rock that's covered in moss. ❏

♥ **Rafiki's Planet Watch:** Conservation Station is a Hidden Mickey paradise with more than 20 Mickeys in the entrance mural alone. Two favorites: Just inside the building on the right, find a possum with a

Hidden Mickey in its eye, then look above it to find a butterfly with two Hidden Mickeys (one on each wing). For good measure, here's a third: Find a frog just to the right of an alligator on the left wall, then find Mickey's smiling face under the frog's right eye. ❑

❤ **DinoLand U.S.A.:** Find the two large dinosaurs holding up a "Chester & Hester's Dino-Rama" sign near the TriceraTop Spin ride. Stand directly underneath the sign and close to the blue dinosaur. A dark blue Hidden Mickey is on the wrist of this dino. Then head to the dig site area of DinoLand, where two hard hats and a fan combine to form another H.M. ❑

❤ **Tree of Life:** A Hidden Mickey made of moss is on the front of the Tree of Life just to the right of the tiger and to the left of the buffalo. Although you may be able to spot it from several vantage points, the best place is right when you enter Discovery Island and before the path splits to Africa and DinoLand. ❑

❤ **Dinosaur:** Before you travel back in time, your ride vehicle passes a laboratory scene on the left (the vehicle actually stops here for a second to give you plenty of time to look). Search carefully to find a blue Hidden Mickey drawn on the lower left corner of a whiteboard. ❑

❤ **Festival of the Lion King:** Look for a bird-house in the queue area beside the theater. The entrance is Mickey-shaped. ❑

❤ **It's Tough to be a Bug!:** This is one of the more challenging Hidden Mickeys to locate, but cast members are happy to help you spot it if you need help. After you enter the "underground" room with all the silly musical posters (but before entering the main theater), find the other entrance to the far side of the room. Now look at the far left wall. This well-concealed (but very cool) Hidden Mickey is hiding in the shadows. ❑

*\* Specifics may change during 2010.*

# Animal Kingdom Dining

Should you find yourself without reservations to a table-service eatery, grab a bite at one of our favorite quick-service establishments. The list* of such spots includes the following:

**ANANDAPUR LOCAL FOOD CAFES:** Located in the Yak & Yeti neighborhood in Asia, these windows proffer sweet and sour pork, shrimp lo mein, crispy honey chicken, burgers, egg rolls, chicken fried rice, and more.

**DINO DINER:** The menu is by no means extensive, but if you're in the mood for a hot dog, popcorn, or a frozen carbonated beverage, you're in luck.

**FLAME TREE BARBECUE:** Head here for wood-roasted barbecue sandwiches and platters. Sample the mild, tomato-based sauce or the spicy, mustard-based one with your smoked beef, brisket, pulled pork, and ribs. Smoked turkey sandwiches and salads are served, too. Can't find the place? Follow your nose.

**KUSAFIRI COFFEE SHOP & BAKERY:** The bakery near Tusker House provides a steady stream of fresh-from-the-oven breakfast treats and assorted desserts, plus cappuccino and espresso.

**PIZZAFARI:** Individual pizzas are available plain and with pepperoni. Other options include Caesar salad and hot Italian-style sandwiches.

**RESTAURANTOSAURUS:** Themed as a campsite for student paleontologists, this fossil-filled space offers burgers, veggie burgers, chicken salad, hot dogs, chicken nuggets, soft drinks, and beer.

**TAMU TAMU REFRESHMENTS:** Stop here for sandwiches and burgers on multigrain buns, chef's salad, cheesecake, milk shakes, and soft drinks.

**TRILOBITES:** Turkey legs and chicken wings . . . what's not to love? Soft drinks are served, too.

* Note that while all of the above participate in the Disney Dining Plan, Pizzafari and Kusafiri Coffee Shop & Bakery are the only places listed here that offer breakfast items.

# Water Parks

## Typhoon Lagoon

This watery playground was inspired by an imagined legend: A typhoon hit a tiny resort village many years ago, and the storm—plus an ensuing earthquake and volcanic eruption—left the village in ruins. The locals, however, were resourceful and rebuilt their town as this "wateropolis."

The centerpiece of Typhoon Lagoon is a huge watershed mountain known as Mount Mayday. Perched atop its peak is the *Miss Tilly*, a marooned shrimp boat originally from Safen Sound, Florida. *Miss Tilly*'s smokestack erupts every half hour, shooting a 50-foot plume of water into the air.

The surf lagoon is huge: Thrilling slides snake through caves, tamer ones offer twisting journeys, and tiny slides entertain small kids. And the Crush 'n' Gusher "water coaster" is a blast. Note that children under age 10 must be accompanied by an adult.

**SURF POOL:** The main swimming area contains nearly three million gallons of water, making it one of the world's largest wave pools. The Caribbean-blue lagoon is surrounded by a white-sand beach, and its main attraction is the waves that come crashing to the shore every 90 seconds. The less adventurous can loll about in two relatively calm tide pools, Whitecap Cove and Blustery Bay.

### CASTAWAY CREEK:

This 2,100-foot circular river that winds through the park offers a lazy, relaxing orientation to Typhoon Lagoon. Tubes may be borrowed for free and are the most enjoyable way to make the trip along the three-foot-deep waterway. The

ride takes guests through a rainforest, where they are cooled by mists and spray, through caves and grottoes that provide welcome shade on hot summer days, and through an area where "broken" pipes from a water tower unleash showers on helpless passersby. There are exits along the way, where guests can hop out for a while and do something else. It takes 20 to 35 minutes to ride around the park without taking a break.

### CRUSH 'N' GUSHER:

This "water coaster" thrill ride is one of a kind. In it, daredevils are whisked along a series of flumes and tossed and turned as they weave through an abandoned tropical fruit factory. There are three spillways to choose from: Banana Blaster, Coconut Crusher, and Pineapple Plunger.

### GANGPLANK FALLS, KEELHAUL FALLS, AND MAYDAY FALLS:

These white-water rides offer guests a variety of slippery trips, two of them in inner tubes. All of the slides course through caves and waterfalls, and past rockwork, making the scenery an attraction in itself. Gangplank Falls gives families a chance to ride together in a three- to five-passenger craft.

### HUMUNGA KOWABUNGA:

These three speed slides, reported to have been carved into the landscape by the historic earthquake, will send guests zooming through caverns at speeds of 30 miles per hour. The 214-foot slides each offer a 51-foot drop, and the view from the top is a little scary. But it's over before you know it, and once-wary guests hurry back for another try. Guests are also warned that they should be free of back trouble, heart conditions, and other physical limitations to take the trip. Guests must be at least 4 feet tall to ride any of the Humunga Kowabunga speed slides. Pregnant women are not permitted to partake.

**KETCHAKIDDEE CREEK:** Open only to those 4 feet tall or under, this area has small rides for pint-size visitors. Children must be accompanied by an adult. There are slides, fountains, waterfalls, squirting whales and seals, a mini-rapids ride, an interactive tugboat, and a grotto with a veil of water that kids love to run through.

**SHARK REEF:** Guests borrow snorkel equipment for a swim through a coral reef, where they come face-to-face with sharks and fish. The reef is built around a sunken tanker. The sharks, by the way, are passive members of the species (leopard and bonnethead). Everyone must shower before entering. Guests must be older than age 5 to experience Shark Reef. Kids under 10 must be accompanied by an adult.

**STORM SLIDES:** The Jib Jammer, Rudder Buster, and Stern Burner body slides send guests off at about 20 miles per hour down winding fiberglass slides, in and out of rock formations and caves, and through waterfalls. It's a somewhat tamer ride than Humunga Kowabunga, but still offers a speedy descent. The slides run about 300 feet, and each offers a different view and experience.

**SURFING:** Surf clinics are available on select mornings before the park opens. For information, call 407-WDW-SURF (939-7873).

## Essentials

**WHEN TO GO:** Typhoon Lagoon gets very crowded early in the day. Hours vary seasonally, but the park is generally open from 10 A.M. to 5 P.M., with extended hours in the summer months. All of the pools are heated in the winter. Note that this park is usually closed for refurbishment during certain winter months. The park may also close due to bad weather. Call 407-824-4321 for updates.

**EXTRA MAGIC HOUR:** Typhoon Lagoon may open one hour early for guests staying in a Disney-owned-

and-operated hotel (plus the Hilton on Hotel Plaza Boulevard) provided that they can prove it and have a valid ticket. The park may stay open three hours later for these guests one night a week during the 2-week Easter period and in the summer.

**HOW TO GET THERE:** Bus service begins from all resorts approximately one hour before Typhoon Lagoon opens for the day. The buses stop at the water park and then at the Downtown Disney Marketplace before 10 A.M. After 10 A.M., resort buses stop at the Marketplace and then Typhoon Lagoon. Buses stop running to the water park about one hour after it closes. Parking is free.

**LOCKER ROOMS:** Restrooms with showers and lockers are located close to the entrance. Other restrooms are available farther into the park. Small lockers cost $10, plus a $5 deposit, to rent for the day, while large lockers cost $12, plus a $5 deposit. Towels rent for $2; life jackets and tubes are available free of charge.

**WHERE TO EAT:** Both Typhoon Lagoon restaurants offer similar fare and outdoor seating. Leaning Palms, which was known as Placid Palms before the typhoon hit, was renamed to fit its somewhat unorthodox architecture. Burgers, pizza, salads, ice cream, and assorted snacks are sold here. Typhoon Tilly's Snack Shack serves chicken tenders, wraps, barbecued pork sandwiches, and ice cream. Let's Go Slurpin' offers frozen drink specialties and spirits. Guests may bring their own food or enjoy fare from the restaurants in designated picnic areas. Alcoholic beverages and glass containers may not be brought into the park. Coolers are allowed.

**FIRST AID:** A first-aid station capable of handling minor medical problems is located just to the left of Leaning Palms.

**BEACH SHOP:** Singapore Sal's, located near the park's main entrance, is set in a ramshackle building left a bit battered by the typhoon. Swimsuits, sunglasses, hats, towels, sunscreen, souvenirs, water shoes, and Typhoon Lagoon logo products are available.

# Blizzard Beach

A wintry, watery wonderland, Blizzard Beach is said to be the result of a freak storm that dropped a mountain of snow onto Walt Disney World, prompting the quick construction of Florida's first ski resort. When temperatures soared and the snow began to melt, designers prepared to close the resort. But when they spotted an alligator sliding down the slopes, they realized that they had created an exhilarating water adventure park.

The slalom and bobsled runs became downhill waterslides. The ski jump is one of the world's tallest (120 feet) and fastest (60 miles per hour) free-fall speed slides.

The centerpiece of Blizzard Beach is the snow-capped Mount Gushmore and its Summit Plummet. Most of the more thrilling runs are found on the slopes of this mountain, which tops out at 90 feet. At the summit, swimmers have a choice of speed slides, flumes, a white-water raft ride, and an inner-tube run. Guests may reach the top of Mount Gushmore via chairlift. The lift has a gondola for guests with disabilities. There are stairs, too.

This is the most action-packed Disney water park yet, with enough activities for the entire family to fill at least a day. Note that kids under the age of 10 must be accompanied by an adult.

**CROSS COUNTRY CREEK:** This meandering 3,000-foot waterway circles the entire park. A slow current keeps visitors moving merrily along. Inner tubes, which are free, are the most pleasant way to travel. The ride includes a trip through a bone-chilling ice cave, where guests are splashed with the "melting ice" from overhead.

**DOWNHILL DOUBLE DIPPER:** Guests travel down these two parallel 230-foot-long racing slides at speeds of up to 25 miles per hour. The partially enclosed water runs feature ski-racing graphics, flags, and time clocks. You must be 48 inches tall to ride.

**MELT-AWAY BAY:** This one-acre pool at the base of Mount Gushmore is equipped with its own wave machine. There are no tsunamis here, however—just a pleasant, bobbing wave.

**RUNOFF RAPIDS:** On this inner-tube run, guests careen down three twisting, turning flumes in a single or double tube.

**SKI PATROL TRAINING CAMP:** An area designed specifically for preteens, Frozen Pipe Springs looks like an old pipe and drops sliders into eight feet of water. The Thin Ice Training Course tests agility as kids try to walk along broken "icebergs" without falling into the water. Snow Falls's "wide" slides allow a parent and child to ride together. At the Ski Patrol Shelter, guests grab on to a T-bar for an airborne trip. At any point in the ride they can drop into the water below. Ski patrol participants also experience Cool Runners, where riders can count on hurtling and whirling over lots of moguls on twin inner-tube slides. No bunny slopes for these brave daredevils.

**SNOW STORMERS:** A trio of flumes descends from the top of the mountain. Guests race down on a switchback course that includes ski-type slalom gates.

**SLUSH GUSHER:** This relatively tame, double-humped waterslide offers a brisk journey through a snow-banked mountain gully. Topping out at 90 feet, Slush Gusher is the tallest slide of its kind. You'll find it on Mount Gushmore, next to Summit Plummet. Guests must be at least 4 feet tall to ride.

**SUMMIT PLUMMET:** The thrilling (and scary!) ride begins 120 feet in the air on a platform 30 feet above the top of Mount Gushmore. Brave souls travel about 60 miles per hour down a 350-foot slide. Near the top, guests pass through a ski chalet. To those watching from below, riders seem to disappear into an explosion of mist. You must be at least 4 feet tall to take the plunge.

**TEAMBOAT SPRINGS:** The longest family white-water raft ride in the world takes six-passenger rafts down a twisting, 1,400-foot series of rushing waterfalls.

**TIKE'S PEAK:** A kid-size variation of Blizzard Beach, this attraction features miniature versions of Mount Gushmore's slides and a snow-castle fountain play area. To enter this zone, adults must be accompanied by a child under four feet tall.

**TOBOGGAN RACERS:** An eight-lane waterslide sends guests racing over a number of dips. They lie on their stomachs on a mat and travel headfirst down the 250-foot route.

## Essentials

**WHEN TO GO:** As a guest favorite, Blizzard Beach tends to get very crowded early in the day. Hours vary seasonally, but the park is generally open from 10 A.M. to 5 P.M., with extended hours in summer. All pools are heated in winter. Blizzard Beach is often closed for refurbishment during certain winter months. It may also close due to inclement weather. For schedules, call 407-WDW-PLAY (939-7529).

**EXTRA MAGIC HOUR:** Blizzard Beach may open one hour early for guests staying in a Walt-Disney-World-owned-and-operated hotel (plus the Hilton on Hotel Plaza Boulevard), provided that they can prove it and have a valid ticket.

**HOW TO GET THERE:** Blizzard Beach is served by the buses that go to and from Animal Kingdom. There is service to and from Epcot and Disney's Hollywood Studios, as well. Parking is free.

**LOCKER ROOMS:** There are restrooms with showers near the main entrance. Other restrooms and dressing rooms are located around the park. Small lockers cost $10, plus a $5 deposit for the day, while large lockers cost $12, plus a $5 deposit. Towels rent for $2, and life jackets and tubes may be used for free.

**WHERE TO EAT:** Burgers, hot dogs, fruit salads, and drinks are available at Lottawatta Lodge, in the main village area. Two snack stands with limited offerings are located in more remote areas: Avalunch and The Warming Hut. Polar Pub offers drink specialties and spirits. There are picnic areas for those who prefer to pack their own food. Alcoholic beverages and glass containers may not be brought into the park. Coolers are allowed.

**FIRST AID:** Minor medical problems are handled at this station near the main entrance.

**BEACH SHOP:** The Beach Haus stocks bathing suits, T-shirts, shorts, sunglasses, hats, sunscreen, beach towels, and more.

# WE'RE GOING TO DISNEY WORLD!
## A DAY-BY-DAY TRIP TRACKER

## DAY 1

_____

**Date**

. . . . . . . . . . . . . . . . . . . . . . . . . . . . . . . . . . . . .

**Flight Information**

. . . . . . . . . . . . . . . . . . . . . . . . . . . . . . . . . . . . .

**Our Resort and Confirmation Number**

. . . . . . . . . . . . . . . . . . . . . . . . . . . . . . . . . . . . .

**Park We Plan to Visit Today**

. . . . . . . . . . . . . . . . . . . . . . . . . . . . . . . . . . . . .

**Dining Reservations**

. . . . . . . . . . . . . . . . . . . . . . . . . . . . . . . . . . . . .

**Notes**

# WE'RE GOING TO DISNEY WORLD!

## DAY 2

_____
**Date**

. . . . . . . . . . . . . . . . . . . . . . . . . . . . . . . . . . .

**Park We Plan to Visit in the Morning**

. . . . . . . . . . . . . . . . . . . . . . . . . . . . . . . . . . .

**Park We Plan to Visit in the Evening**

. . . . . . . . . . . . . . . . . . . . . . . . . . . . . . . . . . .

**Dining Reservations**

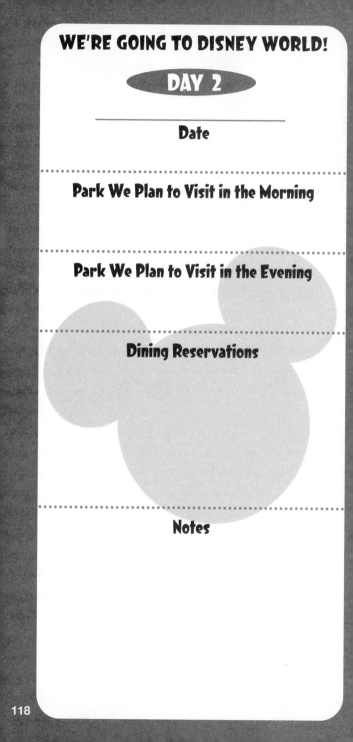

. . . . . . . . . . . . . . . . . . . . . . . . . . . . . . . . . . .

**Notes**

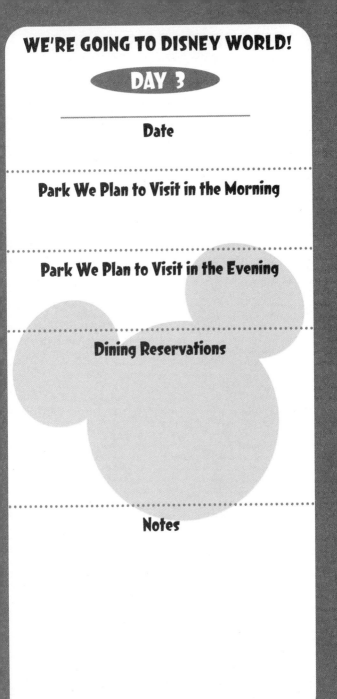

# WE'RE GOING TO DISNEY WORLD!

## DAY 3

**Date**

**Park We Plan to Visit in the Morning**

**Park We Plan to Visit in the Evening**

**Dining Reservations**

**Notes**

# WE'RE GOING TO DISNEY WORLD!

## DAY 4

_____

**Date**

**Park We Plan to Visit in the Morning**

**Park We Plan to Visit in the Evening**

**Dining Reservations**

**Notes**

# WE'RE GOING TO DISNEY WORLD!

## DAY 5

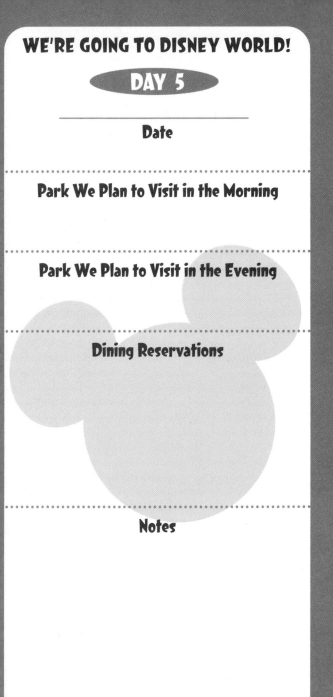

_____
**Date**

**Park We Plan to Visit in the Morning**

**Park We Plan to Visit in the Evening**

**Dining Reservations**

**Notes**

# WE'RE GOING TO DISNEY WORLD!

## DAY 6

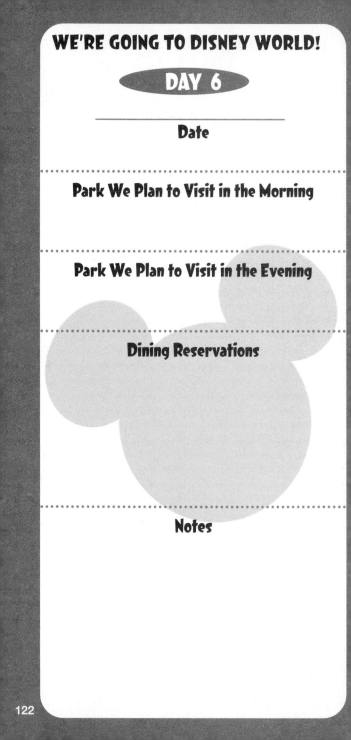

_____

**Date**

**Park We Plan to Visit in the Morning**

**Park We Plan to Visit in the Evening**

**Dining Reservations**

**Notes**

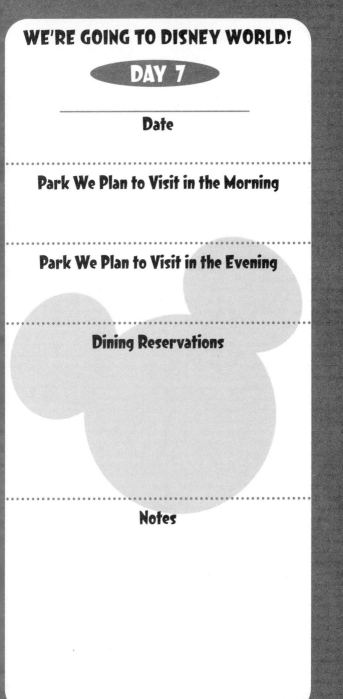

# WE'RE GOING TO DISNEY WORLD!

## DAY 7

_____
**Date**

**Park We Plan to Visit in the Morning**

**Park We Plan to Visit in the Evening**

**Dining Reservations**

**Notes**

# WE'RE GOING TO DISNEY WORLD!

## OUR LAST DAY

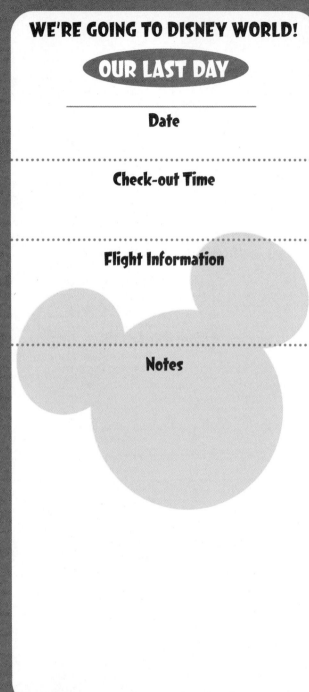

**Date**

**Check-out Time**

**Flight Information**

**Notes**

# INDEX

# Magic Kingdom

## One-Day Schedule

- Welcome to Walt Disney World's original theme park! Be sure to pick up a Times Guide and park guidemap as you pass through the turnstiles.

- Begin the day with a brisk stroll down Main Street, U.S.A. Cut through Adventureland on your way to Splash Mountain and Big Thunder Mountain Railroad. Backtrack to Pirates of the Caribbean, Jungle Cruise, The Magic Carpets of Aladdin, or The Enchanted Tiki Room—Under New Management.

- Access Frontierland via the path near the Tiki Room. Consider lunching at Pecos Bill Cafe or Columbia Harbour House.

- If time allows, squeeze in The Haunted Mansion before the afternoon parade. Watch the parade and move on to Fantasyland. (But visit The Haunted Mansion first.)

- See as much of Fantasyland as possible, including Mickey's PhilharMagic, It's a Small World, Peter Pan's Flight, and The Many Adventures of Winnie the Pooh.

- Cool off at Ariel's Grotto in Fantasyland. If the timing's right, head to the front of the castle for a stage show.

- Explore Mickey's Toontown Fair. Take daring kids on The Barnstormer mini coaster. As a calmer choice, hop on the railroad. Then tour the country homes of Mickey and Minnie Mouse. Mickey greets guests in the Judge's Tent.

- If the evening parade is scheduled to run twice, explore Tomorrowland during the early showing. See (the new-and-improved) Space Mountain, Buzz Lightyear's Space Ranger Spin, Stitch's Great Escape, and the race cars at the Speedway.

# Magic Kingdom

- View Wishes—a truly impressive fireworks display—from Main Street, about halfway between the Train Station and the Castle.

- Watch the nighttime parade from Frontierland.

- If there's time, revisit your favorite attraction (guests are usually admitted right up until closing time).

## IF YOU HAVE YOUNG CHILDREN

- Head directly to Fantasyland (walk right through the castle) and ride Dumbo, Peter Pan, Mickey's PhilharMagic, and The Many Adventures of Winnie the Pooh. Take fans to meet Ariel in her grotto and romp at Pooh's Playful Spot.

- Go to Toontown Fair to meet Mickey in the Judge's Tent. Explore Toontown and stop for a spin in a teacup on the way to Frontierland.

- Check the schedule for the Castle stage show before riding the carrousel and It's a Small World.

- Line up for the afternoon parade about 30 minutes early. Or skip the parade, finish up Fantasyland, and take a magic carpet ride in Adventureland.

- Most little ones enjoy the Walt Disney World Railroad and the Tomorrowland Transit Authority, too.

## LINE BUSTERS

*Even when the park is packed, there are some attractions with shorter or faster-moving lines. Among them*: Tomorrowland Transit Authority, Walt Disney World Railroad (with stops in Tomorrowland, Frontierland, and Main Street, U.S.A.), The Enchanted Tiki Room—Under New Management, Carousel of Progress, Country Bear Jamboree, and Tom Sawyer Island. Of course, we recommend using Fastpass as often as possible!

# Epcot

## One-Day Schedule

- Pick up a Times Guide and park guidemap as you pass through the turnstiles.

- Start the day by making a beeline for Future World's Soarin' and Test Track. Get a Fastpass for one and stand in line for the other. (If the Test Track line is long, consider jumping on the "single riders" line. It moves faster.) If you have no health issues and no susceptibility to motion sickness, experience the out-of-this-world adventure known as Mission: SPACE. (Otherwise ride "Mission: SPACE-lite"—the "less intense," non-spinning version.) Follow it up with the Universe of Energy and The Seas with Nemo & Friends. Keep in mind that World Showcase doesn't open until 11 A.M.

- Stop for lunch at The Land's Sunshine Seasons or Garden Grill, or the Coral Reef restaurant in The Seas with Nemo & Friends pavilion.

- After exploring The Land, be sure to see Honey, I Shrunk the Audience in the Imagination! pavilion (though it frightens small children). Save time to enjoy ImageWorks, a small, high-tech playground.

- If you're in the mood for some serious pin trading (or shopping), stop by Pin Central in Innoventions Plaza. All workers—aka cast members—who are wearing pins are willing to trade. Disney pins only, please.

- Visit Spaceship Earth before visiting Innoventions. And check out the Project Tomorrowland post-show area—it's a blast.

- Make your way to World Showcase by the afternoon and start your tour of the world at Canada. Pick up a "Kimmunicator" on the way (see page 60). Don't miss

# Epcot

the Impressions de France film in the France pavilion and the show in The American Adventure pavilion. Take kids to Gran Fiesta Tour Starring The Three Caballeros in Mexico, and, if there's time, the Maelstrom attraction in Norway.

• After dinner, scope out a spot to watch IllumiNations: Reflections of Earth. (We enjoy the areas near Italy and Japan, but there are excellent viewing locations all around the lagoon.) The Showcase Plaza area (on the Future World side of World Showcase) tends to be the most congested.

Timing Tip: If you have reservations for dinner at World Showcase, give yourself 30 to 40 minutes to get there from the front gate. Taking a *FriendShip* water taxi can shave a few minutes off your trip (although it isn't much faster than brisk walking).

## IF YOU HAVE YOUNG CHILDREN

• Begin the day by thoroughly exploring The Seas with Nemo & Friends. Then head over to Imagination! to experience Journey Into Imagination with Figment and ImageWorks (skip Honey, I Shrunk the Audience—it scares little ones silly).

• At World Showcase, head to Mexico's boat ride and, for braver tots, Norway's Maelstrom. Visit the Kidcot Funstop at each country. Don't miss the koi pond in Japan and Germany's tiny village.

## LINE BUSTERS

*Tired of long lines? Go to*: The Circle of Life movie in The Land, Universe of Energy, or The American Adventure. The Spaceship Earth line thins out in the afternoon. If you don't mind busting up your party, head for Test Track's single riders' line.

# Disney's Hollywood Studios

## One-Day Schedule

- Pick up a Times Guide and park guidemap as you pass through the turnstiles.

- Some attractions open later in the morning; consult the Times Guide specifics. Also, many shows here run on a schedule; check for times throughout the day. Note that this park is not the easiest to navigate. You'll need a map to get your bearings beyond the Chinese Theater.

- Daredevils should begin the day with Rock 'n' Roller Coaster, followed by some eye-opening drops at The Twilight Zone™ Tower of Terror. (We recommend getting a Fastpass for one and standing in line for the other.) Do not ride either on a full stomach!

- They don't call it Toy Story *Mania* for nothing—fans are maniacally devoted to it. Get a Fastpass—early!

- If Beauty and the Beast is playing soon, grab a seat. Otherwise, plan to come back and go to The Magic of Disney Animation or Voyage of The Little Mermaid.

- Pause for lunch at the Sunset Ranch Market or Starring Rolls Cafe.

- Line up 20 to 30 minutes early to watch the Block Party Bash parade. (If you skip the parade, it is a great time to visit Toy Story Mania, Voyage of The Little Mermaid, or The American Idol Experience.)

- Be sure to see (and hear) Sounds Dangerous, followed by the Studio Backlot Tour, Star Tours, Muppet*Vision 3-D, Lights, Motors, Action—Extreme Stunt Show, and the Indiana Jones Epic Stunt Spectacular.

- Make a point of taking tots to the Honey, I Shrunk the Kids Movie Set Adventure.

# Disney's Hollywood Studios

- If you haven't hit it yet, head to The American Idol Experience. Warm up your vocal cords on the way!

- If you missed Beauty and the Beast—Live on Stage, go now. And it's always nice to revisit a favorite show or attraction.

- If Fantasmic is being presented today, you want to get a spot for it at least 60 minutes before show-time. Note that if you choose to skip Fantasmic, plan to exit the park before the performance breaks. If you do stay for the show, know that you can meander through select shops while the throngs file through the turnstiles at the exit.

## IF YOU HAVE YOUNG CHILDREN

- Begin with Toy Story Mania, followed by the Voyage of The Little Mermaid (but warn kids about moments of darkness and a thunderstorm) followed by a visit to Muppet*Vision 3-D.

- Have lunch at Pizza Planet, then watch the parade. Romp in the Honey, I Shrunk the Kids Movie Set Adventure, catch a show at Playhouse Disney, and see Beauty and the Beast—Live on Stage. Skip Fantasmic—it tends to terrify tots. (Mickey's nightmares are central to the plot.)

## LINE BUSTERS

*When lines abound at the Studios, we suggest checking out the following*: Indiana Jones Epic Stunt Spectacular and Lights, Motors, Action— Extreme Stunt Show (both theaters hold thousands of guests at a time), Honey, I Shrunk the Kids Movie Set Adventure, and the American Film Institute Showcase. The Great Movie Ride and Studio Backlot Tour tend to have shorter lines than do their neighboring attractions. Same goes for The Magic of Disney Animation. It's worth looking into.